Complete Guide

to

Home Canning

Alice James

Appreciation from the depth of my heart

I hope this message finds you well and enjoying your latest empowering adventure. I am reaching out to express my deepest gratitude for choosing to embark on this journey with one of my books. Your support by purchasing and reading my book means the world to me.

As an independent publisher, every reader's experience is incredibly valuable. Your decision to invest in my work not only encourages me to continue creating but also plays a vital role in shaping the reading experience for others. Your feedback is a treasure that not only helps me grow as a writer but also assists fellow readers in making informed choices.

If you have a moment, I kindly request you to share your thoughts on your recent reading experience by leaving a review on Amazon. Your honest feedback is not only appreciated but will also be instrumental in guiding future readers in their decision-making process.

Once again, thank you for your support. I am grateful to have you as part of this culinary journey.

Warm regards,

Alice James

Table of Content

Introduction

Dive into the world of homemade goodness with the "Complete Guide to Home Canning," where every jar tells a story, and the kitchen becomes a haven of traditions. Picture this: the aroma of ripe strawberries filling your kitchen, the vibrant hues of freshly picked produce, and the satisfying pop of a sealed jar. Home canning isn't just a skill; it's a journey of flavor and a legacy of warmth.

Let's kick off with a memory we can all savor. Picture a frosty morning, a jar of ruby-red strawberry jam, and the warmth spreading with each spoonful. That's the magic we're tapping into – the joy of creating moments you can taste.

Now, imagine my journey – years in the kitchen, honing the craft of home canning. It's not just about preserving; it's about elevating. My journey is your journey, and together, we'll explore the art and science behind perfect preserves.

Home canning is more than a process; it's a passion. It's about embracing the wholesome, the authentic, and the homemade. As we embark on this culinary expedition, I want you to know it's not just a guide; it's a companion. From the basics to the nuanced, we're delving into a world where your kitchen becomes the canvas, and each jar, a showpiece.

What sets this guide apart is its simplicity and practicality. No jargon, just straightforward advice. I promise you'll not only understand the "hows" but also the "whys." Ever wondered why Grandma's pickles tasted different? We're unveiling those secrets, making sure your creations rival the classics.

I get it. Canning might feel like a leap, but worry not. We're breaking it down step by step. Safety? We've got that covered. Curious about experimenting with flavors? That's what makes this exciting. This isn't just a guide; it's your trusted kitchen companion.

I won't spill all the beans (or should I say, all the pickles?) just yet. Get ready for surprising tips, unique twists, and a journey that unfolds one jar at a time. It's not just about preserving fruits; it's about preserving memories, moments, and the essence of homemade.

Let's embark on this journey together. Because in our kitchens, traditions are born, memories are made, and every jar tells a story.

Welcome to the "Complete Guide to Home Canning," where your culinary adventure begins.

Chapter 1

Unveiling the Art of Home Canning

The history and evolution of home canning

Hey there, fellow canning enthusiasts! Welcome to the heart and soul of home canning, where we're about to embark on a flavorful journey through time. Get ready to dig deep into the roots of this incredible art form, from the humble beginnings to the modern magic happening in your very own kitchen.

It's way back when, and our ancestors were figuring out how to make their harvest last. Home canning didn't start with fancy gadgets and high-tech gear; it was born out of necessity and ingenuity. Back in the day, folks were preserving fruits, veggies, and all sorts of goodness using simple techniques. They relied on pickling, fermenting, and drying to keep the bounty of the season alive beyond its natural lifespan. It was a game-changer, ensuring that every bit of hard work put into growing and harvesting wasn't in vain.

Fast forward to today, and we've taken the canning game to a whole new level. It's not just a survival tactic; it's a passion, an art form, and a celebration of flavors. The history of home canning has seen a beautiful evolution — from grandma's pantry stocked with jars of pickles to your kitchen buzzing with creativity and endless possibilities. As time rolled on, canning methods became more refined. Enter Nicholas Appert, the OG canning maestro. This French inventor cracked the code on sealing food in airtight jars, revolutionizing the preservation game in the early 19th century. His legacy paved the way for the canning revolution we're part of today.

Canning wasn't always the streamlined process we know today. It used to be a bit rough around the edges, relying on trial and error. But oh, how far we've come! We've transitioned from rudimentary preservation methods to a world of precision and innovation. The shift from traditional techniques to modern methods didn't happen overnight. It's a story of continuous improvement, learning from mistakes, and embracing new technologies. Now, we've got the science down to a T, ensuring our canned creations are not just tasty but safe too.

Home canning isn't just about extending the shelf life of your favorite fruits and veggies. It's a statement, a commitment to self-sustainability. As canners, we're not just preserving food; we're preserving a way of life. Think about it – by canning at home, you're reducing your reliance on store-bought goods. You're taking charge of what goes into your pantry, knowing every jar is a testament to your efforts and values. It's a small yet powerful step towards a more self-sufficient and sustainable lifestyle. Let's talk impact. Home canning isn't just about filling jars; it's about making a mark on the world of food preservation. The ripple effect of our canning endeavors goes beyond our kitchen shelves.

When you preserve your own food, you're saying no to excessive packaging and food waste. You're contributing to a greener planet, one jar at a time. It's a subtle but significant shift that resonates with the growing movement towards mindful consumption.

And there you have it – a sneak peek into the rich history and evolution of home canning. We've come a long way from ancient preservation methods to the sophisticated artistry of modern canning.

The transformative journey from traditional preservation methods to modern techniques

Let's take a stroll down memory lane, shall we? Imagine your grandma's pantry, filled with jars of goodness that seemed to defy time. Those were the days of traditional preservation, where folks relied on age-old wisdom to keep the flavors alive. It was a simpler time, and those jars held a treasure trove of memories and deliciousness.

Now, fast forward to today. We've taken that rustic charm and amped it up with a dash of modern flair. Home canning is no longer just about preserving; it's about transforming the way we interact with our food. It's a journey that turns tradition into a culinary adventure, where the past meets the present, and the result is nothing short of mouthwatering. In the good ol' days, preserving was a hands-on affair. Grandma knew the secrets of sealing in freshness, and every jar was a signature to her skill. But hold on to your canning tongs because we've taken that wisdom and added a sprinkle of innovation.

Traditional preservation was all about patience and simplicity. Canning, pickling, and jamming were time-honored traditions passed down through generations. It was about knowing when to harvest, how to pack the jars just right, and creating a symphony of flavors that would linger on the palate. Enter the modern era, where canning is both an art and a science. We've harnessed the power of technology without losing the soul of traditional methods. From precision heat control to vacuum sealing, we've got an arsenal of techniques that would make even the most seasoned canner nod in approval. It's not just about preserving; it's about elevating the entire experience.

Now, you might be wondering, why go through the trouble of this transformative journey from the traditional to the modern? It's about more than just flavors – it's about transforming the way we connect with our food. Home canning is a bridge that spans generations, connecting the simplicity of the past with the innovation of the present. In every jar, there's a story. Whether it's a recipe handed down through the family or a newfound concoction born out of experimentation, each jar is a vessel for memories. It lets us capture the essence of a moment and savor it long after the ingredients have been harvested.

Embracing modern techniques isn't about abandoning tradition; it's about enhancing it. It's the joy of discovering new flavors, experimenting with ingredients, and pushing the boundaries of what's possible. The transformative journey is an invitation to play with your food in the most delightful way.

As we unpack the transformative journey, remember that it's not just about jars on a shelf – it's a lifestyle. Home canning is an ode to the past, a celebration of the present, and a nod to the future. It's a journey that transforms not just our kitchens but the way we view food, flavors, and the art of preserving.

Highlighting the importance of home canning in fostering self-sustainability

Let's start by diving into the rich history of home canning. Our ancestors, armed with simple techniques, preserved the goodness of their harvests to ensure they had a tasty, nutritious stash during lean times. It's a tradition that's stood the test of time, evolving into the modern marvel that is home canning.

Think about it — we've come a long way from grandma's old recipe cards. Home canning has transformed into a dynamic and efficient process, blending traditional wisdom with cutting-edge methods. It's not just about preserving food; it's about embracing innovation while cherishing our culinary roots. Now, let's get to the heart of the matter — why does home canning matter in today's world? Beyond the delicious jars lining your pantry, home canning is a powerful tool for self-sustainability. It puts you in control of what goes into your food, reducing reliance on store-bought, mass-produced items. It's a small yet impactful step towards a more sustainable and independent lifestyle.

Ever heard of Nichola Appert? If not, buckle up, because this guy is the hero of home canning. Back in the early 19th century, he cracked the code on preserving food in sealed glass jars, laying the groundwork for what we now know as canning. His legacy is more than just historical — it's the cornerstone of our journey towards self-sustainability. As we explore Appert's legacy, see the connections between his innovations and our modern canning practices. His pioneering spirit is alive and well in every jar we seal, reminding us that the journey towards self-sustainability is deeply rooted in the past.

So, why bother with home canning in the first place? It's more than just a culinary adventure — it's a lifestyle that champions self-sustainability. As we crack open the lid on the world of home canning, keep in mind that every jar you seal is a step towards a more independent and resilient way of life. Get ready to savor the flavors of self-sustainability — one jar at a time. Happy canning!

The impact of canning on food preservation

The aroma of ripe fruits, the crispness of just-harvested vegetables, and the anticipation of savoring those flavors year-round. That, my friend, is the magic of food preservation. It's a journey that spans generations, from the time when our ancestors discovered the art of keeping food fresh to the present-day innovations that take canning to new heights.

Back in the day, our ancestors mastered the art of preserving food using simple yet effective methods. Smokehouses, drying racks, and root cellars were their go-to tools. It was about making food last longer without compromising on taste, ensuring that a bountiful harvest could sustain them through the lean months. Now, let's fast forward to a time when canning took center stage. The impact was nothing short of transformative. No longer bound by the seasons, canning allowed us to capture the essence of peak freshness and seal it in a jar. Suddenly, the crisp crunch of a summer cucumber or the burst of sweetness from a ripe peach wasn't confined to a specific time of year – it was a pantry staple.

Canning isn't just about preventing spoilage; it's about preserving the very essence of flavor. The impact is felt in every jar – from the zingy kick of a pickled pepper to the comforting warmth of a homemade tomato sauce. It's a culinary journey that transcends time, allowing us to savor the best of each season, whenever we please. At its core, home canning is a celebration of tradition. It's about honoring the wisdom of our forebearers who, with patience and skill, preserved the harvest for the days ahead. The impact of tradition is evident in the familiarity of a well-made jam or the comforting taste of pickled beets – each jar a testimony to the legacy of those who came before us.

But hold on, because tradition doesn't mean staying stuck in the past. Enter modern techniques – the superheroes of the canning world. Pressure canners, vacuum sealers, and precise temperature control have joined our kitchen arsenal, taking the impact of canning to a whole new level. It's not a departure from tradition; it's an evolution that amplifies the flavors we hold dear.

Canning isn't just about preserving food; it's also about preserving memories. Each jar is a time capsule, capturing the essence of a particular moment – the laughter of a family gathering, the joy of a successful harvest, or the shared experience of crafting something delicious together. The impact is felt not just on the palate but in the heart. Think of canning as your personal art studio. With jars as your canvas and ingredients as your paint, you have the power to create culinary wonders. The impact of canning isn't just on the food – it's on the way we view ingredients. Suddenly, a basket of berries isn't just fruit; it's the potential for a delectable spread of jams, jellies, or preserves.

The Legacy of Nichola Appert

Nichola Appert's pioneering contributions to food preservation

Close your eyes for a moment and transport yourself to 19th-century France. Here, in the quaint town of Massy, lived a man whose passion for preserving food would change the culinary landscape forever. Nichola Appert, a name that might not be as familiar as the jars in your pantry, but one that deserves a spotlight in the canning hall of fame.

Nichola Appert wasn't just a culinary enthusiast; he was a preservation maverick. Back in the early 1800s, when refrigerators were but a dream and canned goods a novelty, Appert embarked on a journey that would transform the way we think about food preservation.

Imagine a world without the convenience of popping open a jar of pickles or enjoying the sweet simplicity of canned fruits. In Appert's time, spoilage was the arch-nemesis of food preservation. Appert, however, armed himself with ingenuity and a thirst for knowledge. In his quest to conquer spoilage, Appert discovered the magic of heat. Through meticulous experimentation, he realized that sealing food in airtight containers and subjecting them to controlled heat could keep the nasties at bay. This process, known as *appertization*, was revolutionary. It wasn't just about preserving; it was about sealing in freshness and flavor, creating a culinary excellence.

As we crack open the lid on Appert's legacy, it's essential to recognize the principles that continue to shape our canning practices today. The man wasn't just about sealing jars; he was about understanding the science behind it. Appert's meticulous approach to heat, his understanding of the role of air, and his appreciation for the craft of preservation are the cornerstones of home canning. Ever wondered why your grandma insisted on precise measurements or why that water bath is non-negotiable? Thank Appert. His legacy lives on in every meticulous step of our canning journey. The way we select jars, the care we take in cleaning and sterilizing, and the attention we give to the heat treatment – it's all a nod to the principles laid down by the father of food preservation.

Before Appert, food storage was a tricky business. Preserved goods often suffered from spoilage and were a far cry from the flavors of their fresh counterparts. Appert changed the game. Suddenly, households could enjoy the bounty of summer fruits in the dead of winter. Food wasn't just preserved; it was transformed into something that could be savored year-round.

Appert's work didn't go unnoticed. The French government, recognizing the potential impact on military rations, offered a handsome reward for his breakthrough. The stage was set for the canning revolution to take center stage. Appert's techniques spread like wildfire, and soon, homes around the world were echoing with the satisfying pop of jars being sealed. As we celebrate the marvels of home canning, it's impossible not to tip our canning hats to Nichola Appert. His legacy isn't confined to history books; it lives on in the hum of pressure canners, the click of mason jar lids, and the joy of cracking open a jar filled with preserved goodness.

The next time you twist open a jar of homemade goodness, take a moment to appreciate the pioneer behind the technique – Appert. In every jar of pickles, jam, or sauce, there's a whisper of his ingenuity. It's not just about food preservation; it's about honoring the spirit of innovation that continues to shape our canning adventures.

Theories and principles that laid the foundation for modern home canning

Appert's kitchen – a buzzing hub of activity, with pots simmering and ideas brewing. He wasn't just about cooking; he was on a mission to understand the secrets of food preservation. Spoilage, the arch-nemesis of every homemaker and cook, needed a formidable opponent. And so, Appert set out to crack the code.

Appert's first big revelation? Airtight containers were the unsung heroes of food preservation. By sealing food in containers, he discovered that he could protect it from the harmful effects of air – the invisible villain that led to spoilage. It sounds simple, right? But in that simplicity lay the key to transforming canning from a hit-or-miss endeavor to a reliable preservation technique. As Appert toiled in his kitchen laboratory, he stumbled upon the second piece of the puzzle – heat. Controlled heat, to be precise. By subjecting his sealed containers to the right amount of heat, he found a way to thwart the spoilage process. It was a culinary serendipity that turned jars into time capsules, preserving the freshness and flavors of their contents.

With these foundational principles in hand, Appert formalized his process, giving birth to what we now call *appertization*. It wasn't just a cooking technique; it was a preservation revolution. Theories became practices, and practices became recipes for success. Suddenly, the uncertainty of food preservation gave way to a method that was as reliable as it was innovative.

Appert wasn't just a cook; he was a scientist in the kitchen. He emphasized the need for precision in measurements and timing. Every jar sealed in his kitchen bore the stamp of meticulousness. It wasn't about guesswork; it was about understanding the principles and applying them with care. The patience he infused into the process became a hallmark of successful home canning.

As we explore the theories that laid the foundation for modern home canning, it's essential to recognize how these principles have evolved. What started as a single chef's exploration has transformed into a collective knowledge base, passed down through generations of canners. Appert's principles aren't set in stone; they're more like the notes in a culinary harmony. Each canner brings their own flair, experimenting with heat, adjusting for altitude, and fine-tuning the process to suit their kitchen rhythm. It's a living, breathing evolution that pays homage to Appert's pioneering spirit.

In today's bustling kitchens, Appert's legacy lives on. The importance of creating airtight seals remains a guiding light for canners. Choosing the right jars, inspecting for cracks or defects, and ensuring a snug fit with lids and bands – it's all part of the journey, paying homage to the principles that started it all. Heat remains the guardian against spoilage, just as Appert discovered centuries ago. Whether you're immersed in the gentle simmer of water bath canning or feeling the pressure of a canner at work, it's all about letting heat work its magic. The precise temperature and time echo the principles set forth by the culinary maestro himself.

As we conclude our exploration of Appert's theories and principles, take a moment to look at your pantry shelves. What do you see? It's not just jars of preserved goodness; it's a testimonial to the impact of theories turned into practice. Every jar of pickles, every can of tomatoes – they're not just preserved; they're a culinary triumph, made possible by the foundational principles we've uncovered.

Connecting Appert's legacy to the current landscape of home canning

Picture yourself in the midst of a bustling kitchen. The aroma of bubbling jams and the rhythmic hum of a pressure canner fill the air. Now, let's take a stroll back in time to Appert's kitchen – a place where curiosity and culinary experimentation collided. As we connect the dots between then and now, it's not just about preserving food; it's about preserving a legacy. Appert's legacy isn't a distant echo from the past; it's a living thread that weaves through the fabric of our modern canning practices. In every jar we seal, every lid we tighten, we're not just preserving;

we're participating in a tradition that dates back to a French chef who dared to defy the limitations of his culinary era.

Appert's principles, once confined to the pages of history, have found a home in our kitchens. The concept of sealing in freshness through airtight containers isn't just a vintage idea; it's a cornerstone of modern canning. When we choose the right jars, inspect for defects, and ensure a snug seal with lids and bands, we're not just following a recipe – we're connecting with Appert's ingenious approach to preservation.

As we fire up our canners, whether it's the comforting warmth of water bath canning or the pressure-packed excitement of pressure canning, we're invoking the same guardian against spoilage that Appert discovered centuries ago. The impact of temperature and time, the delicate balance that transforms ingredients into preserved showpiece – it's consonance that echoes the principles laid down by the culinary pioneer.

Appert wasn't just about cooking; he was about precision and patience. In the rush of our modern lives, where time seems to slip away, these principles still hold their ground. From meticulous measurements to the careful timing of heat treatment, we're not just following steps; we're honoring the legacy of a chef who believed that the journey of preservation was as important as the destination.

But Appert's legacy isn't frozen in time. It's evolved into a concinnity of modern canning techniques. We've added new notes – from sous vide canning to innovative approaches in pickling. The principles remain, but the tune has expanded, allowing every canner to find their rhythm in the kitchen orchestra.

As we explore the theories and principles that laid the foundation for modern home canning, we're not just exploring techniques; we're embarking on a culinary adventure. Appert's legacy transcends the kitchen; it's a mindset that encourages us to view canning not just as a necessity but as an exploration of flavors, a celebration of tradition, and a nod to the endless possibilities that lie within every jar.

Appert wasn't just a preservationist; he was an innovator. As we experiment with flavor combinations, explore unconventional pickling methods, and push the boundaries of what's possible in our home kitchens, we're not just canning; we're embracing the spirit of innovation that Appert introduced to the culinary world.

Understanding USDA Guidelines

Overview of the USDA's role in setting canning standards

Ready to dig into the nitty-gritty of home canning standards? In this section, we're shining a spotlight on the unappreciated hero that ensures our canned goods are not just delicious but safe – the USDA. So, grab your canning gear, and let's explore the role of the USDA in setting the standards that keep our home-canned creations top-notch.

Before we unravel the mysteries of USDA guidelines, let's get to know the United States Department of Agriculture (USDA) a bit better. Think of them as your canning guardian angels – experts who've got your back in ensuring that the jams, pickles, and sauces on your pantry shelves are not just tasty but also safe for consumption. The USDA isn't just a bunch of bureaucrats pushing papers; they're the safety net that prevents canning adventures from turning into culinary misadventures. Their role? To establish guidelines that help us avoid the pitfalls of unsafe canning practices. It's not about stifling creativity; it's about providing a reliable roadmap for canners to navigate.

See the USDA as your culinary compass, guiding you through the canning wilderness with three essential markers – *quality, safety, and nutrition.* These are the pillars that uphold their guidelines. It's not just about canning for the sake of it; it's about creating canned goods that stand tall on these three principles. The USDA understands that the essence of canning isn't just about preventing spoilage; it's about preserving the very soul of flavor. Their guidelines emphasize the importance of selecting top-notch ingredients, maintaining proper sanitation, and employing techniques that ensure your canned goods are a burst of quality in every bite.

Now, let's talk safety – the heartbeat of USDA guidelines. The last thing you want is a jar of pickles turning into a potential health hazard. The USDA provides canners with the golden rules of heat treatment, jar sanitation, and processing times to ensure that harmful microorganisms are kicked out of the canning party. It's about avoiding foodborne illnesses; and at the same time, canning with confidence.

The USDA doesn't just stop at flavor and safety; they're also concerned about the nutritional value of your canned creations. Their guidelines steer canners toward practices that retain the goodness of vitamins and minerals in the canning process. So, when you crack open a jar of home-canned tomatoes, you're not just savoring flavor – you're getting a nutritional boost Imagine embarking on a canning journey without a compass. It could be a bit like wandering in the dark, right? The USDA is that guiding star for home canners. Their guidelines aren't restrictive rules; they're a *North Star*, helping you navigate the complexities of canning with confidence.

One thing to note is that USDA guidelines aren't carved in stone. They're more like a well-worn recipe card that occasionally gets a tweak for the better. The USDA stays on the pulse of canning science, continually updating their recommendations to reflect the latest in food safety and preservation. So, as a canner, you're not just following rules; you're staying in sync with the evolving landscape of food safety.

Now, let's zoom in a bit. When it comes to canning methods, the USDA plays referee, ensuring you choose the right play for the right game. Water bath canning and pressure canning – each has its domain, and the USDA helps you understand when to whip out the water bath and when to bring in the pressure canner.

Fruits, pickles, and high-acid delights – that's the territory of water bath canning. The USDA lays out the guidelines, making sure your jams and jellies are as safe as they are scrumptious. It's not just about dunking jars in hot water; it's about understanding the nuances that make water bath canning a culinary ballet. On pressure canning – the superhero of low-acid foods like vegetables, meats, and soups. The USDA provides canners with the playbook for pressure canning, ensuring that every low-acid creation in your pantry is a safe and savory masterwork. It's not just about the hiss of the pressure canner; it's about embracing the guidelines that turn it into your culinary ally.

While the USDA is your co-pilot in the canning journey, it's crucial to recognize that the responsibility isn't entirely off your shoulders. As a canner, staying informed is your superpower. The USDA provides the guidelines, but it's your keen eye, attention to detail, and commitment to safe practices that ensure your home-canned goods are a source of pride, not concern.

Think of canning as a dynamic duet between you and the USDA guidelines. They set the stage, providing the script for safe and delicious canning practices. You, the canner, bring the passion, creativity, and commitment to the kitchen. It's a partnership that ensures every jar you seal is a validation to the magic of home canning.

As we wrap up this exploration of the USDA's role in setting canning standards, let's take a moment to appreciate the wisdom they bring to our canning kitchens. It's not just about rules and regulations; it's also about canning with confidence, knowing that the guidelines are there to empower, not restrict.

Significance of staying informed about the latest USDA-approved methods

Home canning is like a dance – a rhythmic harmony of ingredients, heat, and jars. And, like any dance, it evolves. Enter the USDA – your dance instructor, guiding your steps in the ever-changing world of safe food preservation. Staying informed about their latest methods isn't just about keeping up; it's about leading the dance with confidence

Let's get real for a moment. The canning landscape is a dynamic one, with new research, technologies, and insights pirouetting onto the stage regularly. Being in the know isn't about being a canning scholar; it's about ensuring your culinary prowess remains not just graceful but also safe. Imagine trying out a new move without knowing the rhythm – staying informed is your way of swaying through the canning dance floor with confidence.

Now, let's talk about the essence – the significance of staying informed about the latest USDA-approved methods. It boils down to two words: *safety and flavor*. USDA-approved methods aren't just about preventing spoilage; they're your insurance policy against potential hazards lurking in improperly preserved foods. It's not a matter of sacrificing flavor for safety; it's about ensuring your flavorful creations are backed by the seal of safety.

Canning isn't a static science; it's a dynamic one that waltzes hand in hand with evolving technologies and scientific breakthroughs. Staying informed about the latest USDA-approved methods is your ticket to being at the forefront of this culinary tango. It's not just about following the steps; it's about understanding the rhythm, embracing the melody, and creating a canning excellence that stands the test of time.

Now, let's peel back the layers and unveil the significance of staying informed. It's not just a formality; it's your assurance that every jar you seal is a masterpiece of safe preserving. Whether you're a seasoned canner or just starting, the latest USDA-approved methods are your compass, guiding you through the canning wilderness and ensuring you emerge with jars of culinary triumph.

Canning, at its core, is a voyage into the unknown – a journey where you transform raw ingredients into delectable delights. Staying informed about the latest USDA-approved methods is like having a shield against the unknown. It's your defense against potential pitfalls, ensuring your culinary adventure is one of joy and not of unforeseen challenges.

One of the key aspects of staying informed is understanding the secrets of heat treatment. The USDA-approved methods demystify the world of temperatures and processing times, ensuring that harmful microorganisms are not just invited but kicked out of the canning party. It's not about boiling jars for the sake of it; it's about knowing the precise temperature dance that renders your creations safe.

Ever wondered why the type of jars, lids, and rings matters? The latest USDA-approved methods spill the beans. It's not just about aesthetics; it's about creating a hermetic seal that keeps your goodies safe from the elements. The USDA guidelines are your manual for selecting the right tools – ensuring your jars aren't just vessels but guardians of flavor.

Staying informed isn't just about following guidelines; it's about adapting to innovations. Canning technologies are ever-evolving, and the USDA is your beacon in this sea of change. From sous vide canning to novel pickling techniques, the latest methods are your passport to exploring the uncharted territories of home preservation. It's not about being resistant to change; it's about embracing the canning renaissance with open arms. In the world of canning, tradition and modernity waltz hand in hand. Staying informed allows you to strike the perfect balance. You're not abandoning time-tested practices; you're enhancing them with the latest knowledge. It's about respecting the roots of canning while allowing the branches to stretch toward new horizons.

As a canner, you're not just a cook; you're a maestro orchestrating a concord of flavors. With this title comes a responsibility – a responsibility to stay informed. The USDA provides the score, but it's your skilled hands and discerning palate that transform the notes into a culinary masterpiece. It's not just about following steps; it's about leading the orchestra with confidence.

Canning isn't a one-time skill; it's an art of continuous learning. Staying informed about the latest USDA-approved methods is your brushstroke of knowledge on the ever-expanding canvas of home preservation. It's not about reaching a destination; it's about relishing the journey, with each jar filled being a testament to your commitment to excellence.

Chapter 2

Essential Equipment and Tools

Selecting the Right Tools

Choosing appropriate canning jars, lids, and bands

From jams that burst with the essence of summer berries to pickles that capture the crispness of garden cucumbers – the right jars are your partners in preserving flavors. But how do you choose the perfect canvas for your edible artwork?

Canning jars come in various shapes and sizes, each with its unique charm. From the classic Mason jars to the sleek quilted versions, your choice depends on the culinary showpiece you envision. Pint jars for those small-batch experiments, quart jars for the family-favorite sauces – it's like picking the right brush for your artistic expression.

Now, let's talk about the dynamic duo – lids and bands. They're not just accessories; they're your culinary sidekicks, ensuring that every jar is a tightly sealed treasure trove of goodness. Choosing the right lids and bands is not about aesthetics; it's about the science of creating a hermetic seal that locks in flavor and freshness.

Lids come in different materials – metal and plastic. Metal lids are like the sturdy knights guarding your preserves, creating a reliable seal. Plastic lids, on the other hand, are the flexible acrobats, perfect for non-canning purposes like storing dried herbs. Your choice depends on the nature of your culinary quest.

Bands, also known as screw bands, are the apparel that hold everything together. They're like the supporting characters in a novel, ensuring a tight plot twist in your canning journey. When it comes to bands, choose the ones that match your lids – they're like the perfect dance partners, moving in sync to create a canning masterpiece.

In the sphere of canning, quality tools are not a luxury; they're a necessity. Think of them as your trusted allies in the quest for perfectly preserved flavors. Quality jars resist breakage, quality lids create airtight seals, and quality bands ensure a snug fit. It's not about being fancy; it's about setting the stage for a canning adventure free from mishaps.

Jars come in various materials – glass and plastic. Glass jars are the classics, allowing you to showcase the vibrant colors of your creations. Plastic jars, on the other hand, are like the modern rebels, perfect for on-the-go snacks or picnics. Your choice depends on the intended use and the aesthetic you want to achieve.

Let's break it down further. For jams, jellies, and sauces, go for pint-sized jars. They're like the solo performers, shining bright with concentrated flavors. For pickles, fruits, and large-batch wonders, quart-sized jars are your go-to. They're the ensemble cast, each ingredient playing a vital role in the canning drama.

Remember, lids and bands are not one-size-fits-all. Match the size of your lids with the size of your jars. It's like finding the perfect pair of shoes – not too tight, not too loose. When it comes to bands, ensure they're rust-free and in good condition. They're like the reliable anchors in your canning sea.

Exploring options for canners, including water bath and pressure canners

Imagine the water bath canner as the expert leading the beginner's journey of canning. It's like the gentle conductor guiding you through the basics of preserving fruits, jams, and high-acid goodies. This canner is your entry ticket into the world of home canning – a place where flavors are sealed with simplicity and tradition.

So, when does the water bath canner take center stage? When you're preserving high-acid foods, like fruits, tomatoes, and pickles, this tool shines. It's like the gentle hug that cradles your jars in a warm bath, ensuring that the contents are safely sealed without compromising their vibrant flavors. Water bath canning is a culinary ritual – a dance of jars in simmering water, a process that turns the raw into the preserved. It's not just about dunking jars into hot water; it's about orchestrating a gentle ballet where the warmth envelopes your culinary creations, transforming them into time capsules of taste.

Now, let's step into the realm of the pressure canner – the command center for the seasoned canning pro. It's like the superhero cape you wear when venturing into the preservation of low-acid foods, like vegetables, meats, and stews. The pressure canner is your ticket to a world where hearty soups and savory sauces are preserved with prowess.

The pressure canner takes the stage when you're dealing with low-acid delights. It's like the vigilant guardian that ensures harmful microorganisms are vanquished in the heat, leaving your jars of goodness safe for future feasts. When it's time to elevate your canning game beyond the basics, the pressure canner steps into the limelight. Pressure canning is a bit like culinary chemistry – the transformation of ordinary ingredients into shelf-stable wonders. It's not just about sealing jars; it's about harnessing the power of pressure to reach temperatures that ensure the annihilation of potential spoilers. The pressure canner is your magical cauldron, turning raw ingredients into long-lasting treasures.

Now, let's talk about the choice between the water bath and pressure canner. It's not a battle; it's a duet, each canner playing a distinct role in your culinary exploration. The water bath canner is like the opening act, setting the tone with its simplicity and ease. It's perfect for beginners and for preserving high-acid delicacies.

As your canning journey evolves, the pressure canner steps in. It's like the rising crescendo in your culinary voyage, taking you to the next level of preservation. When you're ready to tackle low-acid foods and venture into the world of hearty soups and savory stews, the pressure canner becomes your indispensable partner.

Choosing between a water bath and pressure canner isn't a conundrum; it's a show of practicality. Consider the nature of your culinary creations. Are you drawn to the bright flavors of fruits and pickles, or are you eager to explore the savory depths of meats and vegetables? Your choice depends on the rhythm of your kitchen and the flavors you wish to preserve.

Think of water bath and pressure canners as the multifaceted tools in a chef's arsenal. They're not just vessels; they're gateways to a world of culinary diversity. The water bath canner is like the gentle breeze that carries the scent of fruits in summer, while the pressure canner is the gust of wind that brings the hearty aroma of a simmering stew.

Proper care of your canners ensures their longevity, allowing them to be reliable partners for years to come. It's not about complicated maintenance; it's about simple rituals that keep your canning tools in top-notch condition. After each culinary performance, give your canners a little love. It's not about meticulous scrubbing; it's about ensuring that they're free from residue and ready for the next act. A gentle wash with mild soap and water is all it takes to keep them shining.

Just like any seasoned performer, your canners may show signs of wear and tear over time. It's not a cause for panic; it's an opportunity for a little TLC. Inspect seals, valves, and gauges for any signs of damage, and replace worn-out parts as needed. This ensures that your canners continue to perform at their best.

Importance of quality tools for successful home canning

In the field of home canning, jars, lids, and bands aren't just vessels; they're the main tools that carry the legacy of flavors preserved. Picture them not as mere tools but as partners in your culinary journey, contributing to the harmony of tastes that unfold in every jar. Let's duck into the essence of quality tools and how they become the silent architects of successful canning.

Quality tools are like the paintbrushes of a culinary artist. Imagine trying to create a masterstroke with subpar brushes – the strokes would lack finesse, and the final result might not capture the true essence of your vision. Similarly, in home canning, quality tools are your brushes, allowing you to craft flavors with precision and passion.

Let's begin with the fabric of your culinary artwork – the canning jar. Choosing the right jar is not just about practicality; it's about recognizing the potential within those glass walls. Quality jars go beyond the basics; they're crafted to withstand the heat of the canning process, ensuring that your preserved delights emerge unscathed and flavorful.

You've spent hours cultivating the perfect batch of homemade jam or pickles. Now, imagine entrusting them to a jar that isn't up to the task. Quality jars, with their sturdy build and tight seals, become the guardians of your culinary creations. They stand as a stamp to your dedication, ensuring that each jar is a treasure trove of flavors waiting to be discovered.

Next in our toolkit are the lids – the unseen protectors of your flavorful treasures. Quality lids aren't just about sealing; they're about creating a hermetic embrace that shields your creations from the outside world. When it comes to preserving the integrity of your jams, jellies, or pickles, the lid isn't merely a closure; it's the final seal of perfection.

Ever opened a jar of preserves only to find it lacking the vibrancy you worked so hard to capture? Blame it on the lid. Quality lids, with their snug fits and reliable seals, preserve the freshness within, ensuring that each jar opened is a burst of flavors as if plucked straight from your garden or kitchen.

Now, let's turn our attention to the humble band – the reliable guardian that holds the symmetry of canning together. Quality bands aren't just about practicality; they're about standing strong in the face of heat and pressure. They secure the jar and lid in a culinary embrace, allowing the magic of preservation to unfold without a hitch.

Consider this: you've meticulously followed a canning recipe, and the time has come to reveal your creation. A subpar band might falter, allowing air to sneak in and compromise your creations. Quality bands, with their robust construction, ensure that the culinary plans play out as intended, with each jar delivering a crescendo of flavors. Imagine your kitchen as a dance floor, and the tools as dance partners moving in perfect harmony. Quality tools don't just participate in the dance; they lead it. They're your choreographers, ensuring that every step in the canning process is executed with finesse and precision.

Quality tools bridge the gap between tradition and innovation. They carry the legacy of time-tested canning practices while embracing modern advancements. In every jar sealed with quality tools, you're not just preserving flavors; you're elevating the art of home canning, becoming a culinary innovator in your own right.

Investing in quality tools is an investment in culinary success. It's not about the price tag; it's about recognizing the value they bring to your kitchen. Quality tools pay dividends in the form of successful canning ventures, where each jar becomes a confirmation to your commitment to preserving flavors with authenticity and care.

Detailed explanation of necessary equipment

Let's kick things off by unveiling the basic tools that lay the foundation for your canning journey.

1. Water Bath Canner:

Description: A large pot with a fitted lid, this bad boy is your go-to for water bath canning. It's like the stage where your jams, jellies, and pickles perform their delicious drama.

Why It's Crucial: The water bath canner ensures your jars get the gentle heat they need to seal the deal, preserving those fruity or savory treasures.

2. Pressure Canner:

Description: A heavy-duty pot with a locking lid and pressure gauge, the pressure canner is your powerhouse for low-acid foods. It's like the heavyweight champion in your kitchen.

Why It's Crucial: When you're diving into veggies, meats, and soups, the pressure canner is your kitchen superhero. It brings the heat and pressure to keep things safe and sound.

3. Canning Jars:

Description: Glass jars with snug-fitting lids—your culinary tool for holding all those mouthwatering creations. They're like the gallery where your pickled art is showcased.

Why They're Crucial: The right jars are your trusty companions, ensuring airtight seals that lock in flavors and keep your goodies shelf-stable.

4. Lids and Bands:

Description: The unsung heroes of canning—flat lids and screw-on bands. They're like the silent protectors, sealing the fate of your culinary masterpieces.

Why They're Crucial: Lids and bands create the airtight seal essential for safe and successful canning. They're your culinary security detail.

Must-Have Utensils - Your Kitchen Allies

Now that we've covered the basics, let's talk about the tools that make the actual canning process a breeze.

1. Jar Lifter:

Description: A handy set of tongs with rubberized grips, your jar lifter is the VIP backstage pass to handling hot jars. It's like the gentle hand that ensures your jars make a safe entrance and exit.

Why It's Crucial: Hot jars and bare hands don't mix. The jar lifter is your heat resistant assistant, allowing you to place and remove jars with ease.

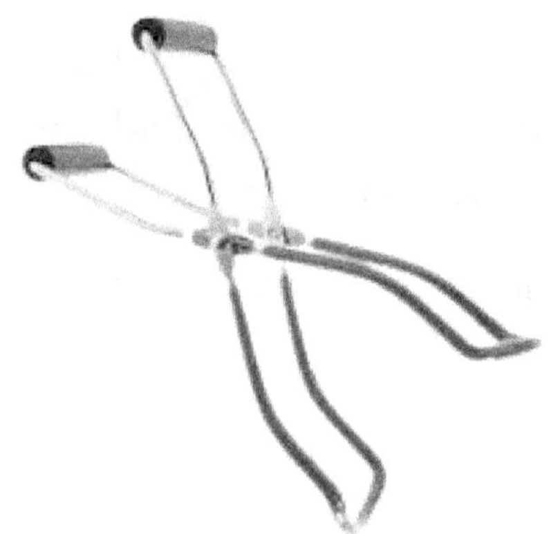

2. Canning Funnel:

Description: A wide-mouthed funnel designed for mess-free filling of jars. It's like the spotlight, directing your culinary creations to take center stage.

Why It's Crucial: Precision matters, especially when pouring hot jams or sauces. The canning funnel ensures your ingredients hit the jar and not the countertop.

3. Bubble Remover and Headspace Tool:

Description: A nifty little tool that's flat on one end and round on the other. It's like the leveler, making sure there's just the right amount of space in your jars.

Why It's Crucial: Creating the perfect headspace prevents messy overflows and ensures proper sealing. This tool is your secret weapon against culinary chaos.

4. Magnetic Lid Wand:

Description: A magic wand for lids, this tool makes grabbing those flat lids a breeze. It's like the magician's assistant, effortlessly producing the finishing touch.

Why It's Crucial: Fumbling with hot lids is a recipe for disaster. The magnetic lid wand ensures a smooth lid application, sealing your jars with a touch of magic.

Thermometers and Timers

Let's not forget the unsung heroes—tools that keep an eye on the temperature and time, ensuring your culinary show hits all the right notes.

1. Canning Thermometer:

Description: A trusty thermometer designed for accuracy in temperature. It's like the conductor, ensuring your canning orchestra hits the right heat levels.

Why It's Crucial: Accurate temperatures are non-negotiable in canning. This thermometer ensures your culinary creations are in tune with safety standards.

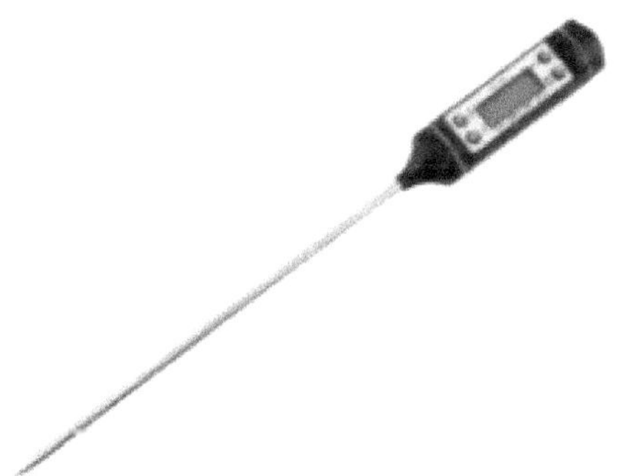

2. Kitchen Timer:

Description: A simple timer with a loud bell, your kitchen timer is the timekeeper, making sure your jams, pickles, and sauces don't overstay their welcome on the heat.

Why It's Crucial: Timing is everything in canning. This timer is your reminder to prevent undercooked or overcooked disasters.

Wrapping It Up - Storage and Labels

Before we conclude, let's talk about what happens after the curtain falls on your canning performance.

1. Cooling Rack:

Description: A simple grid-like rack for placing hot jars post-canning. It's like the backstage lounge where your culinary creations cool down and solidify their flavors.

Why It's Crucial: Rapid cooling is key to sealing the deal. The cooling rack ensures your jars cool evenly, setting the stage for a perfectly preserved performance.

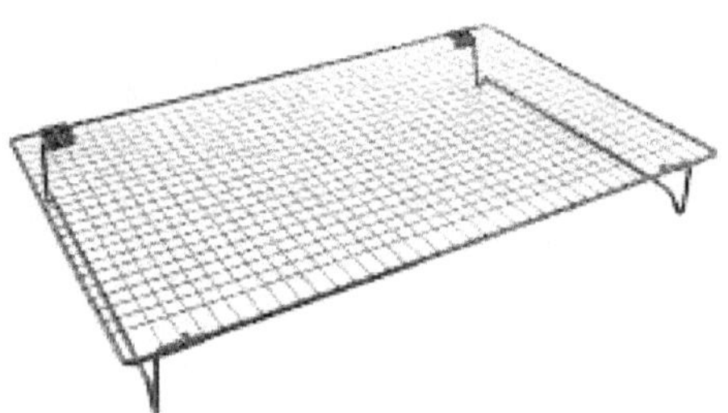

2. Labels and Permanent Markers:

Description: Your tools for labeling and dating your creations. They're like the name tags that ensure you never forget the stars of your pantry.

Why They're Crucial: Organization is your best friend. Labels and markers help you keep track of what's in each jar and when it's time to shine on the culinary stage.

Innovative tools to enhance the canning process

High-Tech Canning Appliances

1. Electric Water Bath Canner:

Description: Imagine your classic water bath canner, but add a dash of electricity. It's like turning up the heat with the flick of a switch.

Why It's a Game-Changer: No more waiting for the water to reach the perfect temperature—this electric wonder gets things boiling faster, saving you time and energy.

2. Smart Pressure Canner:

Description: Your traditional pressure canner, but with a brain. It's like having a kitchen assistant that knows the perfect pressure for every canning masterpiece.

Why It's a Game-Changer: Smart technology ensures foolproof pressure control, taking the guesswork out of canning. It's a safer and smarter way to tackle low acid foods.

Futuristic Canning Jars   Where Style Meets Preservation

1. Vacuum Seal Jars:

Description: Regular jars, but with a twist —vacuum-sealed lids. It's like giving your culinary creations a space-age enclosure.

Why It's a Game-Changer: Vacuum sealing locks in flavors with precision, extending the shelf life of your goodies and keeping them fresher for longer.

2. Reusable Silicone Lids:

Description: Think of your classic metal lids, but made from flexible silicone. It's like giving your jars a cozy, stretchy sweater.

Why It's a Game-Changer: Say goodbye to single-use lids. These reusable marvels not only save the planet but also provide a snug seal for multiple rounds of canning.

Next-Level Utensils - Making Canning Effortless

1. Automatic Jar Lifter:

Description: Your trusty jar lifter, but with an automatic grip. It's like having a robotic hand that delicately handles hot jars.

Why It's a Game-Changer: Perfect for those who want to eliminate the risk of jar slippage. The automatic grip ensures a secure hold, even when things get steamy.

2. Adjustable Canning Funnel:

Description: A traditional funnel, but with adjustable sizing. It's like having a funnel that caters to jars of all shapes and sizes.

Why It's a Game-Changer: Versatility is the name of the game. No more searching for the right funnel size; just adjust and pour, saving you precious time and cleanup hassle.

Cutting-Edge Monitoring Tools - Precision at Your Fingertips

1. Bluetooth-Enabled Canning Thermometer:

Description: A classic thermometer, but with a tech upgrade. It's like having your canning temperatures at your fingertips through your phone.

Why It's a Game-Changer: Monitor temperatures remotely, receive alerts, and ensure your canning process stays on track without hovering over the pot.

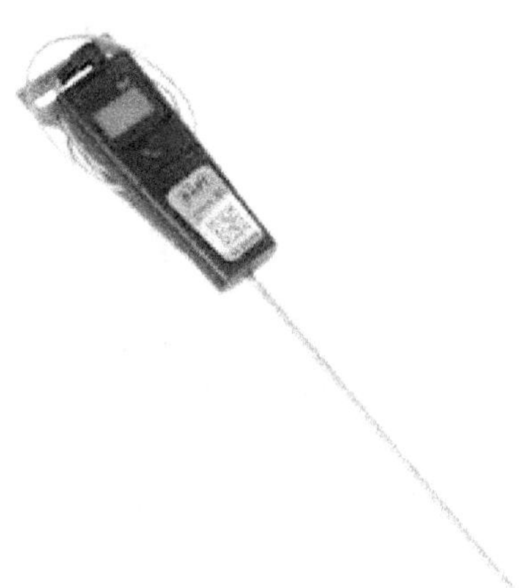

2. Smart Canning Timer:

Description: Your basic kitchen timer, but with a touch of intelligence. It's like having a timer that adapts to your canning recipe, adjusting for altitude and specific requirements.

Why It's a Game-Changer: No more second-guessing if your timer is set right. This intelligent timer customizes itself to your canning needs, ensuring precision without the stress.

Space-Age Storage Solutions - Keeping Your Pantry Neat

1. Stackable Canning Jars:

Description: Regular jars, but designed to nest neatly on top of each other. It's like creating a canning tower of space-saving awesomeness.

Why It's a Game-Changer: Maximize pantry space with stackable jars, creating a visually pleasing and organized display of your preserved treasures.

2. Magnetic Canning Labels:

Description: Labels with built-in magnets. It's like turning your jars into a magnetic poetry board.

Why It's a Game-Changer: Easy label swapping and reorganizing. Move your magnetic labels around without any sticky residue, keeping your pantry Pinterest-worthy.

Creating a personalized toolkit for efficiency

Let's start with the cornerstone of your toolkit – the canning jar. Imagine it as a blank canvas waiting to be adorned with the colors and textures of your culinary creations. Choosing the right jar goes beyond mere practicality; it's about finding a vessel that resonates with your canning spirit.

Consider the size and shape of your jars as the architects of your canning classics. Are you drawn to the quaint charm of half-pint jars for your signature jams? Or do you lean towards the grandeur of quart-sized vessels for hearty soups? Tailor your choice to the recipes that spark joy in your canning repertoire.

Glass or plastic – the choice is yours. Glass jars offer transparency, allowing you to witness the vibrant hues of your preserves. On the other hand, plastic jars bring a lightweight and shatterproof option to the canning stage. Your material choice is a personal touch, a nod to your canning preferences. Next is the silent guardians of flavor – the canning lids. These unassuming discs play a pivotal role in sealing the essence of your culinary efforts. Your choice of lids can be a subtle nod to efficiency, offering a balance between convenience and sustainability.

Are you a one-time canner enthusiast, favoring the ease of single-use metal lids? Or do you lean towards the sustainability tango, opting for reusable lids that promise an encore performance? The choice lies in your canning rhythm, a beat that aligns with your kitchen values. Before the lids take the stage, inspect them for perfection. A smooth surface without dents ensures a flawless seal, guaranteeing that your culinary creations remain locked in until the grand unveiling. It's a simple yet crucial step in the efficiency dance of canning.

Enter the party in unison – the canning bands. These circular companions secure the lids in a tight embrace, setting the stage for a fess canning performance. Your choice between metal and reusable bands adds a personal flair to the efficiency dance.

Metal bands, the classic choice, are like the reliable dance partners who know the steps by heart. Reusable bands, crafted from materials like silicone, bring a modern twist to the canning waltz. The decision is yours – a nod to tradition or a step towards sustainability. Inspect the bands for strength before canning begins. A robust, undamaged band ensures that your lids are held securely in place, ready to face the heat and pressure of the canning process. Efficiency in canning starts with the reliability of your tools.

Now, let's turn our attention to the culinary spectacle – the canner. The choice between a water bath canner and a pressure canner is a reflection of the rhythms in your canning routine. Water bath canners are like the gentle beats of a waltz, perfect for high-acid fruits and pickles. They create an inviting atmosphere for flavors to meld and harmonize. Pressure canners, the passionate tango partners, are ideal for low-acid vegetables and meats, bringing the heat and intensity required for safety.

Consider the material of your canner – stainless steel, enamel-coated steel – as the foundation of your canning process. The size of the canner sets the tempo, ensuring that your jars move and groove comfortably without feeling cramped. A well-matched canner is the key to an efficient and harmonious procedure. Before the grand performance of canning, your tools undergo a backstage ritual – the art of jar sterilization. Picture it as the preparation before the efficiency dance, ensuring that every tool is ready to shine on the culinary stage.

Cleaning jars, lids, and bands is a gentle step. Use hot, soapy water and a brush to waltz away any remnants of past kitchen remains. Sterilization is the tango that follows – boiling, oven, or dishwasher. Choose the rhythm that suits your kitchen beat, aligning with your efficiency goals. After the process, inspect your jars for purity. A smooth, intact rim is the mark of a jar ready to face the world of flavors. This inspection ensures that your jars are fit to stand against contamination, ready to preserve the culinary treasures within.

As you curate your personalized toolkit, think of your tools as an extension of yourself in the efficiency show of canning. The jars, lids, bands, and canners are not just tools; they are co-conspirators in your canning masterpiece.

Crafting a personalized toolkit is not just about having tools; it's about having the right tools that resonate with your canning spirit. Efficiency in canning is not a one-size-fits-all concept; it's a personalized scenario where every tool has a purpose, and every jar tells a story.

Mastering the Art of Jar Preparation

Proper cleaning and sterilization of canning equipment

Here, we're looking into the main steps of preparing your canning equipment — a show of cleanliness and sterilization that sets the stage for the preservation success in your kitchen. Join me as we master the art of jar preparation, ensuring that your tools are not just ready but primed to capture the essence of your culinary creations.

Before the grand canning performance, your jars, lids, and bands enter a pre-show ritual — a soapy prelude that cleanses them of any lingering traces from past culinary acts. Picture it as a gentle waltz with warm, soapy water, where each tool is gracefully swayed in the suds, bidding farewell to the remnants of yesterday's kitchen tales.

Introduce a soft-bristled brush to the canning melody, a partner that swirls and twirls around the curves and corners of your jars. This brush waltz is a meticulous dance, ensuring that no flavor notes from previous performances linger on the surface. It's a simple yet crucial step, setting the tone for a fresh, clean canvas.

After the soapy waltz, inspect your tools for residue-free brilliance. Run your fingers along the surfaces, feeling for any subtle traces left behind. A smooth, clean finish ensures that your jars, lids, and bands are ready to embrace new flavors without a hint of the past.

Now that your tools have had their soapy feel, it's time for the sterilization process. Choose your preferred choice — boiling, oven, or dishwasher. Each method adds its own flair to the efficiency dance, ensuring that your tools are not just clean but sanitized, ready to face the heat of the canning spotlight.

Picture the boiling waltz as the traditional wingman, a reliable partner that has graced kitchens for generations. Submerge your tools in boiling water, letting the bubbles and heat cleanse every nook and cranny. It's a process that withstands the test of time, leaving your tools refreshed and ready for their role in the preservation journey.

For those seeking a modern efficiency jig, the oven method is your perfect choice. Arrange your tools on baking sheets, and let the heat of the oven perform its sterilization magic. It's a quicker tempo, a contemporary twist to the classic boiling waltz, perfect for those with a bustling kitchen rhythm.

If multitasking is your kitchen mantra, the dishwasher cha-cha awaits. Load your jars, lids, and bands into the dishwasher, and let it perform the cleaning and sterilization steps while you focus on other culinary moves. It's a show of convenience, where efficiency meets hands-free brilliance.

After the sterilization tango, inspect your tools for sterilized purity. Run your fingers along the surfaces, feeling for any imperfections. A smooth, sterilized finish is the mark of tools ready to take center stage in the canning spotlight, free from any lingering microorganisms that may disrupt the best of flavors.

As your tools emerge from the sterilization tango, invite them to a final inspection waltz. This is the grand finale, where you run your keen eyes and hands over each jar, lid, and band. Look for any signs of imperfection – a tiny crack, a dent, or any irregularities that might compromise the flawless performance of your tools.

A smooth, intact rhythm is what you're aiming for. The jars should gleam, the lids should be flawless, and the bands should stand strong. This final inspection waltz ensures that your tools are not just clean and sterilized but primed for a flawless performance, ready to capture and preserve the melodies of your culinary creations.

The role of sanitized jars in preventing contamination

Jars, our faithful guardians of flavor, play a pivotal role in preventing contamination. Think of them as the sentinels standing between the purity of your culinary creation and the outside world. The cleanliness of these jars is their armor, shielding the treasures within from any unwanted intruders. Now, as our jars await their moment in the culinary spotlight, they partake in the waltz of sterilization – a process to ward off any unwanted guests. This isn't just about appearance; it's about creating an environment where harmful microorganisms dare not tread.

Imagine the sterilization process as a ballet of heat, where each jar gracefully twirls under the spotlight of boiling water, oven heat, or the rhythmic hum of the dishwasher. This heat ballet isn't just a show; it's a crucial step in ensuring that our jars are not just clean but sanitized to the core.

Now, let's dig into the crucial role of sanitized jars in preventing contamination. Picture these jars as fortresses, their sanitized walls forming a barrier against the unseen invaders that could compromise the integrity of your culinary masterpieces. Contamination, the uninvited guest to our culinary soiree, can take many forms – molds, yeasts, and bacteria, each waiting for an opportunity to sneak into our jars and disrupt the harmonious flavors within. Here, the role of sanitized jars becomes paramount, standing guard to ensure that only the intentional flavors are invited to the feast.

When we sanitize our jars, we are essentially donning them in armor. This armor, forged through the heat ballet, acts as a formidable defense against the microbial foes that may attempt to infiltrate our preserves. It's a shield, ensuring that our jars are not just vessels but guardians of the culinary treasures within. As the jars emerge from their sterilization process, it's time for the final act of assurance – the inspection for purity. Imagine this as a tender embrace, where you run your fingers along the cooled jars, feeling for any imperfections. A smooth surface is the confirmation that your jars are ready to embrace the flavors without a trace of unwanted elements.

In the course of preservation, the role of sanitized jars is like the sweet melody that ties the entire composition together. It ensures that the flavors play harmoniously without any discordant notes introduced by contamination. A smooth, sanitized surface is not just an aesthetic preference; it's the assurance that your culinary creation is protected and preserved.

Tips for inspecting jars for cracks or defects

In the domain of home canning, our jars are not just vessels; they are the instruments that contribute to the collection of flavors we compose in our kitchens. Each jar, like a note in a melody, plays a crucial role. But, as with any method, imperfections may attempt to introduce discord into the composition. Inspecting your jars before they take center stage is akin to tuning your instruments before a performance. It's a moment of mindfulness, ensuring that each jar is ready to contribute its part to the harmony of flavors without any unexpected disruptions.

Now, let your fingers join the operation. Feel the surface of each jar, much like a detective exploring a crime scene. Smoothness is your ally; any unexpected roughness may signal a defect that could lead to trouble during the canning performance. Picture cracks as the silent saboteurs lurking in the wings, waiting for their moment to disrupt the show. A tiny crack may seem inconspicuous, but it has the potential to grow into a major performance spoiler, leading to leaks or even breakage.

Defects, on the other hand, are the culprits of contamination. A flaw in the glass could provide a hiding spot for unwanted microbes, threatening the safety and integrity of your preserved creations.

Tips for Inspection Brilliance

1. Adequate Lighting

Begin your inspection under adequate lighting. Illuminate the stage where your jars will perform. Natural light or a well-lit kitchen counter can be your best accomplice, revealing even the most subtle imperfections.

2. View from Every Angle

Don't let any jar hide in the shadows. Rotate and turn each jar, viewing it from every angle. A defect might reveal itself only when seen from a specific perspective.

3. Consistency Check

Consistency is key in any performance. Run your fingers along the surface, ensuring a smooth ensemble of glass. Any abrupt changes in texture could signify a crack or defect trying to disrupt the seamless harmony.

4. The Sound Test

Engage the sound test. Gently tap each jar with your fingertips, listening for a clear, resonant tone. A dull or uneven sound could indicate a flaw in the glass, an auditory cue that helps you uncover hidden defects.

5. The Magnifying Glass

For a close-up rehearsal, enlist the help of a magnifying glass. It acts as your zoom lens, allowing you to scrutinize even the tiniest details. A magnifying glass is your ally in detecting subtle cracks or defects that might go unnoticed by the naked eye.

If, during the inspection, you discover a jar with cracks or defects, consider it as a dissonant note in your culinary techniques. Discard it without hesitation. Prioritize safety and the integrity of your preserved delights, ensuring that only the jars in perfect shape take their place on the canning stage. With the inspection complete, your jars are now ready for the spotlight.

Quality Ingredients Matter

Selecting the freshest produce for optimal results

The art of choosing

The essence of freshness is the heartbeat of your culinary creations in the arena of home canning. Every jar you fill is a result to the quality of the produce you choose. The journey to optimal results begins in the garden, at the farmer's market, or in the aisles of your local grocery store. This is where you handpick the stars that will shine in your jars.

Let's start our exploration with vibrancy. Picture the colors of the rainbow – the deep reds of tomatoes, the vibrant greens of cucumbers, and the rich hues of berries. Vibrancy is your visual cue to freshness. Choose produce that practically sings with color, promising a palette of flavors that will burst forth in your preserved delights.

Move on to the texture test. Run your fingers over the surface of your chosen produce. Whether it's the crispness of apples or the firmness of peaches, your fingers are the best judges of quality. A firm texture indicates freshness, ensuring that your canned goods will maintain a pleasing bite and texture.

Engage your olfactory senses in the selection process. The aroma of your chosen produce should be like a fragrant overture, promising a scent of flavors. Close your eyes, take a deep breath, and let the scent guide you. A strong, sweet fragrance is the scent of success in the world of canning.

Consider the size of your chosen produce. Optimal proportions matter. For fruits and vegetables alike, choose specimens that are neither too small nor too large. The right size ensures even cooking during the canning process, allowing flavors to meld harmoniously in each jar.

While imperfections in life add character, in the realm of canning, blemish-free beauty is your goal. Inspect your produce for any bruising, cuts, or blemishes. Not only do flawless fruits and vegetables promise optimal taste, but they also minimize the risk of allergies or spoilage.

With your carefully selected produce in hand, it's time to transition from the garden to the canning stage. Envision this as a seamless performance, where the stars of your garden take center stage in each jar. The process of preserving freshness is like capturing a melody in a timeless jar.

The Canning Stage:

Imagine swift transitions – from plucking the ripest tomatoes from the vine to placing them gently into jars. Swiftness is your ally in preserving the essence of freshness. The less time your produce spends in transit, the more vividly its flavors will shine in the final act.

Handle your chosen produce with the care of a maestro conducting a culinary dexterity. Bruises and mishandling can disrupt the natural harmony of flavors. Treat each fruit and vegetable with the gentleness it deserves, ensuring that its freshness is preserved from the garden to the jar.

As you tighten the lids on your jars, envision it as the encore – the celebration of optimal results. Each jar is a testament to your meticulous selection, a bottled brilliance that captures the very essence of the produce you carefully curated.

Consider labeling your jars as a way of notating the content within. Whether it's "Farm-Fresh Peaches" or "Garden-Ripened Tomatoes," let your labels reflect the freshness and origin of the ingredients. It's your way of sharing the backstory of each jar, adding a personal touch to your culinary composition.

With the freshest produce carefully selected and preserved, your culinary masterpiece awaits. Picture a tasting room filled with friends and family, each jar a seal to the vibrant flavors and meticulous care you invested in your home canning journey.

Exploring unique ingredients for creative canning

Just as an artist selects unique pigments to create a classic artwork, you, as a canner, have the opportunity to choose ingredients that will transform your preserved goods into works of culinary art. Here are the steps:

Let's begin our journey with unconventional fruits. Move beyond the usual suspects and explore exotic options that add a surprising twist to your canned goods. Imagine the tangy sweetness of passion fruit in your preserves or the subtle floral notes of lychee dancing on your taste buds. Unconventional fruits open a gateway to a world of undiscovered flavors.

Venture into the realm of heirloom vegetables, each one a heritage of taste. Consider the robust flavors of heirloom tomatoes, the earthy richness of purple carrots, or the vibrant hues of rainbow chard. These unique vegetables not only offer distinct tastes but also contribute to the visual outlook of your canned goods.

Spices are the secret notes in your culinary skill set. Explore exotic spices that elevate your canned creations to new heights. Picture the warm embrace of cardamom in your peach preserves or the subtle heat of star anise in your pickled beets. Spices add layers of complexity, turning each jar into a sensory experience.

Infusions are the spirits of innovation in the world of canning. Consider the depth that a splash of bourbon adds to your cherry preserves or the aromatic infusion of lavender in your apricot jam. These creative touches not only enhance flavor but also provide a delightful surprise with every spoonful.

As you explore these unique ingredients, envision a palette of possibilities laid out before you. The choice of ingredients is your artistic expression, and each jar is a fabric waiting to be adorned with the flavors that resonate with your culinary vision.

Just as a composer balances musical notes, you, as a canner, must balance flavors. Consider the interplay of sweet and savory, the harmony of tartness and richness. Balancing flavors ensures that each jar is a collection of taste, where no single note overwhelms the others.

Creativity thrives in experimentation. Don't be afraid to embrace the unknown and try combinations that defy tradition. Picture the excitement of adding a touch of basil to your blueberry jam or infusing your apple chutney with a hint of chili. These bold experiments are the brushstrokes that create culinary masterwork.

Make each jar uniquely yours by adding a signature touch. Consider the addition of a vanilla bean to your peach preserves or a sprinkle of sea salt on your caramel apple butter. These personal touches elevate your creations from mere recipes to culinary expressions of your individual style.

As you tighten the lids on your jars, visualize it as the final stroke on your culinary act. Each jar is a preserved gem, capturing the essence of your creativity. Share these works of art with friends and family, inviting them to savor the unique flavors you've carefully crafted.

Also, consider labeling your jars not just as a practical necessity but as a way of expressing the story behind each creation. Whether it's "Passionfruit Collection" or "Heirloom Harvest Medley," let your labels be a glimpse into the culinary journey you embarked on to create each unique jar.

Understanding the role of each ingredient in preserving flavor

Let's explore the varieties of elements that transform ordinary fruits and vegetables into culinary wonders.

1. Fruits: Fruits, with their natural sugars and vibrant hues, set the sweet overture of your canned creations. Whether it's the succulent juiciness of peaches or the tartness of berries, each fruit brings a unique melody to your flavor composition. Understand the essence of each fruit, ensuring that its flavor shines through in every spoonful.

2. Vegetables: Vegetables provide the earthy undertones in your canning voyage Think of the robustness of tomatoes in your salsa or the crunch of cucumbers in your pickles. Look into the role of vegetables, balancing sweetness with savory notes and adding depth to your flavor palette.

3. Sweeteners: Sweeteners, like a melodic bind, bring all the elements together. Whether it's the honey in your fruit preserves or the maple syrup in your apple butter, sweeteners harmonize the flavors, creating a cohesive and delightful taste experience.

4. Acids: Acids, the zesty crescendo, add brightness to your canned goods. Citrus fruits, vinegar, or even a splash of wine – these acids elevate flavors, cutting through sweetness and providing a refreshing contrast.

5. Preserving flavor is a delicate dance of balance. Consider the interplay of sweet, savory, tart, and acidic notes. Each ingredient contributes to the equilibrium, ensuring that no single flavor dominates. Understand the delicate art of crafting a harmonious blend that pleases the palate

As we venture into the wizardry of flavor preservation, consider techniques that retain the essence of each ingredient:

a. Cold Pack vs. Hot Pack: Understand how the method of packing influences the texture and taste of your canned goods.

b. Timing Matters: Learn the art of timing in canning – from picking fresh produce at the peak of ripeness to processing jars at the right moment to lock in flavors.

c. Layering Flavors: Just as a chef layers ingredients in a dish, experiment with layering flavors in your jars. Consider the order in which ingredients are packed to create a delightful progression of tastes. The quality of your ingredients is the cornerstone of flavor preservation. Choose the freshest fruits and vegetables, sourced at their peak, to ensure that the flavors you capture in your jars are nothing short of exceptional.

Canning is not just a method; it's a journey of discovery. Embrace experimentation in your flavor laboratory. Try different combinations, tweak recipes, and let your taste buds guide you in creating unique and unforgettable flavor profiles.

Chapter 3
The Science Behind Successful Canning

pH Levels and Recipe Modification

The significance of pH levels in canning

As we embark on our canning journey, let's dive into the fascinating world of the science behind successful preservation. Here, our spotlight is on pH levels—a crucial factor that can make or break the safety and quality of your canned goods. So, let's unravel the mysteries of pH in the art of canning.

pH, or potential hydrogen, is a scale that measures the acidity or alkalinity of a substance. In canning, this scale becomes our guiding compass, influencing the safety and flavor of our preserved delights.

Fruits, particularly those bursting with citrusy goodness, often take the stage with a low pH. The acidity acts as a natural preservative, inhibiting the growth of harmful microorganisms and lending a zesty kick to your jams and preserves. Some vegetables, like tomatoes, gracefully balance on the neutral side of the pH spectrum. Their pH levels make them perfect candidates for canning, offering an opportunity for the creation of versatile sauces and salsas.

While less common in canning, certain vegetables may sway towards the alkaline end. Though pickling these might not be the norm, understanding their pH ensures a safe and delicious performance When canning fruits or vegetables with a less-than-ideal pH, a dash of lemon zest or a splash of vinegar can lead the front towards safer levels. These acidic partners not only enhance flavor but also ensure the microbial safety of your preserves. The delicate balance of pH extends beyond safety to flavor. Adjusting recipes for different acidity levels is akin to a chef fine-tuning a recipe to perfection. Embrace the art of balancing pH to create a taste balance that resonates with your palate.

Think of pH as your safety net in the canning circus. Understanding and manipulating pH levels ensures that harmful microorganisms are kept at bay, providing a secure environment for your canned creations. As the canner, you wield the pH baton, guiding your ingredients through the procedures of preservation. Feel the power in your hands as you confidently modify recipes, ensuring both safety and flavor align harmoniously.

pH levels join forces with heat treatment in a grand ballet against microbial invaders. Together, they ensure that your canned goods are not just safe but also bursting with the natural flavors of your carefully selected ingredients. Furthermore, understanding the pH safety net becomes crucial when dealing with low-acid vegetables or experimenting with unique recipes. Mitigate risks by staying within the safe pH range, allowing your culinary creativity to flourish without compromising safety.

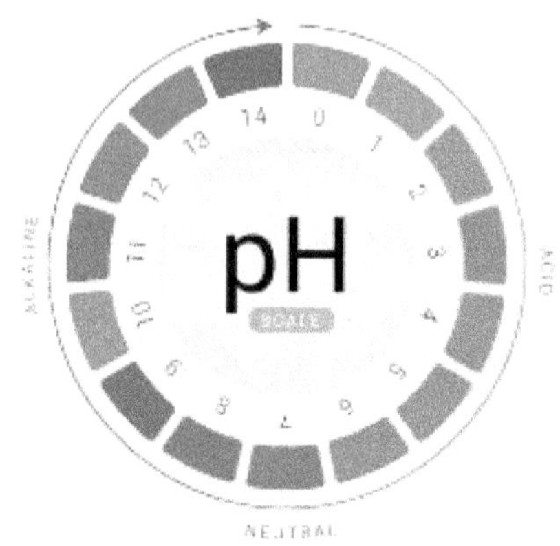

How to adjust recipes for different acidity levels

Citrus fruits, the rockstars of acidity, bring a burst of zing to your preserves. Oranges, lemons, and limes take center stage, infusing your creations with a lively and vibrant acidity. Tomatoes strike a chord of balance. Their acidity, while not as bold as citrus, lends a subtle tang that transforms ordinary sauces into culinary wonders.

As a canner, you're not just preserving; you're conducting a balance of flavors. Understanding the pH spectrum allows you to navigate the acidity scale, ensuring a harmonious balance in every jar.

Adding lemon zest not only elevates the acidity but introduces a coherence of citrusy undertones, enhancing the overall flavor profile. On the other hand, vinegar, a backstage virtuoso, plays a crucial role in adjusting acidity levels. Whether white, apple cider, or balsamic, each vinegar brings its unique note to the culinary composition.

Think of pH as your compass in the acidity wilderness. As you embark on adjusting recipes, let pH be your guide, ensuring that you stay within the safe and flavorful realms of home canning. Much like a tightrope walker, maintaining balance is key. Adjusting acidity levels is a delicate process, and your expertise lies in achieving the perfect equilibrium between safety and taste.

Step outside the conventional and explore innovative infusions. Think jalapeños in your strawberry jam or basil in your peach preserves. Experimentation adds a personal touch to your preserves, creating a flavor masterwork. Your pantry is your palette, and each ingredient adds a stroke of flavor. From spices to herbs, let your creativity run wild as you tailor recipes to suit your taste preferences.

When dealing with low-acid vegetables like beans or carrots, mastering safe modification becomes essential. Adjusting acidity levels ensures that your creations are both safe for consumption and bursting with flavor. The canning kitchen is a realm of innovation, but safety should always be your guiding star. Safely modifying recipes allows you to push the boundaries while keeping your culinary creations well within the safe zone.

Guidance on the safe modification of canning recipes

Home canning is not just a science; it's an art. As you tread the path of recipe modification, envision yourself as a culinary expert, blending safety protocols with your creative instincts to craft unique, flavorful preserves. Think of safety as your guiding compass. Safe recipe modification ensures that your culinary experiments not only tantalize the taste buds but also adhere to the essential principles that make home canning a trusted method of preservation.

When faced with low acid ingredients like vegetables, the procedure becomes more intricate. Safely modifying recipes for low-acid vegetables involves understanding the delicate balance required to preserve both safety and taste. Your canning kitchen is a stage, and each adjustment is a note in the symmetry of flavors. Balancing low-acid ingredients with acidity adjustments ensures a safe yet flavorful performance in every jar.

As you modify recipes, let inspiration be your muse. Infuse your creations with unique combinations, experimenting with flavors that resonate with your taste buds. Whether it's a hint of spice or a dash of herbs, let your palate lead the way.

Safe modification is an art mastered over time. It's about understanding the science behind canning while allowing your culinary intuition to guide the process. Each modification should reflect your personal taste and contribute to the rich tapestry of your canning legacy.

In the field of safe recipe modification, ratios are your allies. Whether adjusting acidity levels or altering ingredient quantities, respecting these ratios ensures a delicate equilibrium between safety and the artistry of canning.

At the core of safe modification lies the preservation of flavors and safety alike. Embrace the principles that make canning a time-honored tradition, weaving the threads of tradition into the fabric of your culinary creations.

Importance of proper heat treatment in destroying harmful microorganisms

Heat is the vigilant guardian of your preserves, standing resolute against microbial intruders. In the canning realm, it's not just about cooking; it's about safeguarding the purity of your creations. Microorganisms lurk in the shadows, waiting to compromise the integrity of your canned goods. Proper heat treatment is the hero that neutralizes this microbial menace, ensuring your jars emerge victorious in the battle against contamination.

Understand the precise temperature requirements for different foods, orchestrating a culinary overture that ensures both safety and flavor merge harmoniously in your jars. Heat treatment is not a sudden blast but a gradual crescendo, allowing the temperature to permeate every nook and cranny of your concoction. This gradual rise ensures that harmful microorganisms succumb to the heat, leaving your preserves pristine.

As canners, we are culinary conjurer, turning raw ingredients into treasures sealed within glass. Proper heat treatment is the catalyst that transforms this enchantment into a ritual of purity, ensuring your canned goods are not just cooked but fortified against microbial invaders. Embrace the scientific correlation of heat and time. Each jar is a unique performance, and your mastery lies in orchestrating the perfect balance to ensure both safety and the preservation of flavors.

Proper heat treatment extends the lifespan of your creations. Your jars are time capsules, preserving the goodness within and allowing you to savor the flavors of each season long after it has passed. Beyond flavor, heat treatment safeguards the nutritional value of your canned goods. It's a dual role—preserving both the essence of taste and the nourishment that makes your creations not just delightful but wholesome.

Heat is your ally, but like any ally, it must be managed with finesse. Strike an equilibrium between safety and flavor, ensuring that your heat treatment neither compromises taste nor leaves room for microbial mischief. As a canning master, infuse your heat treatment with artistry. It's not just about reaching a specific temperature; it's also about conducting a culinary magic that transforms raw ingredients into time-defying delights.

Creative Flavor Combinations

Unique flavor pairings for jams, jellies, and preserves

Have you ever imagined your kitchen as a play park and your jars as the canvas for a culinary blockbuster? Well, get ready to play because we're turning your preserves into a flavor-packed extravaganza. Let's step beyond the ordinary and explore the endless possibilities that extend far beyond the traditional berry brigade. From exotic fruits to unexpected garden gems, we're diving into a sea of flavors that'll redefine your jam game.

Ever thought about the bold ballet of flavors that spices can bring to your preserves? Cinnamon-kissed apple jam or a ginger-infused peach preserve, anyone? Mother Nature provides a treasure trove of flavors, and we're here to help you unlock them. Discover the magic of unique fruit pairings that go beyond the expected. Imagine this: blueberry and lavender jam or a raspberry-rosemary jelly. The possibilities are as endless as your imagination.

Citrus fruits add a zesty flavor to your preserves. From tangy orange marmalade to a lively lemon-lime jelly. Herbs aren't just for savory dishes; they're the secret ingredients that can take your sweet spreads to new heights.

Ready for a culinary tango? Balancing sweetness with a hint of spice can transform your preserves into a taste sensation. Whether you prefer a gentle heat or a spicy kick, we've got the tips to help you find your sweet and spicy equilibrium.

Introducing innovative ingredient choices for pickling and canning

Sure, pickles are fantastic, but have you ever considered the vast array of ingredients beyond cucumbers that you can pickle? It's time to expand your pickling palette and turn ordinary ingredients into extraordinary delights. Think beyond cucumbers; there's a whole world of vegetables waiting to be pickled.

Who says pickling is only for veggies? Pickled fruits add a sweet and tangy twist to your canning repertoire. Pickled peaches with a hint of spice or tangy mango slices – your taste buds are in for a fruity delight! No more basic pickling spice blends – it's time to spice things up! Cumin-infused pickled carrots or coriander-spiced green beans, anyone?

Who said pickles have to be strictly savory? We're breaking the rules and adding a sweet experience to the mix. Sweeteners like honey, maple syrup, or even brown sugar can elevate the flavor profile of your pickled creations.

Balancing sweet and tangy flavors is an art, and we're here to guide you through it. Learn how to create a harmonious blend that will make your taste buds sing. Sweet and tangy bread-and-butter pickles, anyone? Vinegar is a classic, but why stop there? From beer-infused brines to fruity wine concoctions, the possibilities are endless.

Ditch the plain white vinegar and duck into a world of creativity. Apple cider vinegar, rice vinegar, or even balsamic – let's mix it up! Canning is a personal journey, and your palate is the compass. Become the maestro of your pickling adventure!

Herbs and Spices

Exploring the world of herbs and spices in enhancing flavors

Let's talk about pantry—herbs and spices. They're not just there to collect dust; they're the flavor architects of your canned jewel. Imagine turning a regular strawberry jam into a flavor explosion with just a touch of basil, or infusing your peach preserves with the warm embrace of cinnamon.

Before we dive into the pots and pans, let's get acquainted with our herbal friends. This isn't a science class; it's more like making new buddies. Thyme, for instance, has this earthy charm that pairs beautifully with blueberry jams. Rosemary? It's the secret weapon for elevating the sweetness of apricots. Get ready to have an herb garden party in your jars!

Hold on to your canning hats because we're flipping the script. Who said canning is all about sweetness? Picture a tomato and basil jam or a savory spread that rocks your grilled cheese world. We're giving herbs a new job description, and they're embracing the savory side with gusto. Here's the thing about herbs and spices—they are like the spices of life, but for your jars. Too much, and your creation might overwhelm; too little, and it's a flavor snooze-fest.

Don't worry; you don't need a green thumb for this. Even a windowsill can be your herb haven. We're spilling the beans on how to incorporate fresh herbs into your canning game. Imagine the aroma of mint infusing your berry jams or lavender turning your preserves into a fragrant paradise. Fresh herbs—because your jars deserve the VIP treatment.

We're breaking free from the traditional canning cocoon. Ever wondered how cumin could turn your apple chutney into an exotic delight or how lemongrass could zing up your marmalades? This is your ticket to canning without borders, where flavors unite in a global party.

Now, here's the fun part. Tradition is a starting point, not a roadblock. We're giving you permission to play mad scientist in your kitchen. Throw in a little extra thyme, experiment with basil, and let your culinary instincts run wild. This is your kitchen; these are your creations.

Canning is not just about preserving; it's about celebrating the evolving flavors that come from blending tradition and innovation. Your jars aren't just containers; they're storytellers narrating the tale of your unique culinary journey.

Guide on incorporating herbs for savory canning

Alright, let's kick things off by acknowledging the unsung heroes of the savory canning world—herbs. They're not just pretty plants; they're the conductors of a savory flavor that will elevate your canned creations to a whole new level.

It's time to break free from the sweet shackles and explore the savory wonders that herbs can bring to your jars. Think beyond jams; envision pickles, chutneys, and spreads that add a savory kick to your pantry. Basil, oh sweet basil! It's not just for pasta or bruschetta anymore. From tomato and basil jams to basil-infused pickles, your jars are about to get a fragrant upgrade.

Thyme, the often-underestimated herb, is about to take the stage. Learn how to infuse thyme into your savory jams, jellies, and spreads. Picture a thyme-infused onion marmalade that will have you rethinking the possibilities of thyme in your savory canning repertoire. Rosemary isn't just for roasted potatoes; it's here to revolutionize your canned goods.

When it comes to savory canning, it's all about finding the right balance. No one wants a jar that's all thyme and no basil, right?

Ever thought about adding cumin to your pickles or curry to your savory chutneys? Take a trip to the spice aisle and explore how global flavors can turn your savory canning into a cultural delight.

In the world of savory canning, there are no strict rules—only guidelines to help you unleash your inner culinary genius. Experiment with herbs, blend global flavors, and make your jars a testament to your unique taste preferences.

Tips on balancing flavors for a delightful culinary experience

Before we jump into the tips, let's get to know our flavor players. Herbs bring freshness, spices add depth, and your main ingredients provide the star power. Ready to create a great showpiece?

Tip #1: Start Simple, Build Slow

Balancing flavors is an art, not a race. Start with a basic recipe and gradually introduce additional elements. This slow-build approach allows you to savor each note and ensure that no single flavor dominates the jar. Picture it as a gradual crescendo that leads to a flavorful finale.

Tip #2: Know Your Ingredients' Strengths

Just like in any team, each player has strengths. Understand the intensity of your herbs, the punch of your spices, and the natural sweetness or acidity of your main ingredients. This knowledge helps you orchestrate a balanced composition, ensuring no flavor overwhelms the others.

Tip #3: Sweet, Sour, Salty, Bitter, Umami—Embrace the Spectrum

Balancing flavors is like a dance across the taste spectrum. Sweet, sour, salty, bitter, umami—all are partners in this culinary waltz. Experiment with the proportions, and let your palate guide you. A well-balanced jar should hit multiple notes, leaving you with a complex and satisfying taste experience.

Tip #4: The Herb and Spice Tango

Herbs and spices are the dance partners in your flavor tango. Pairing them strategically can elevate your canned products to new heights. Consider classics like basil with tomatoes or rosemary with savory pickles. Let the herbs and spices complement each other, creating a flavorful synergy that resonates in every bite.

Tip #5: The Acidity Waltz

Acidity is like the elegant partner in a waltz—it brings balance and liveliness to the dance. Citrus, vinegar, or even a splash of wine can add that zing that lifts your flavors. Experiment with small quantities at first, ensuring it enhances without overpowering.

Tip #6: Taste as You Go

You're not just a canner; you're the conductor of your flavor voyage. Taste your concoction as you go, adjusting the notes until they hit the perfect harmony. This hands-on approach ensures that your jars reflect your unique taste preferences.

Tip #7: Consider Your Audience

Who are you canning for? Your family, friends, or maybe yourself? Consider the taste preferences of your audience. If they enjoy bold flavors, you can be a bit more adventurous. If subtlety is the key, finesse your flavor balance accordingly. Your culinary skills should resonate with those who savor it.

Tip #8: Document Your Compositions

As a passionate home canner, your flavor experiments are a journey. Keep a flavor journal, noting the combinations that worked wonders and those that need a tweak. This not only helps you recreate successful batches but also serves as a testament to your growth as a flavor maestro.

Water Bath Canning Fundamentals

Step-by-step guide to water bath canning

We're digging into the heart of preservation—the world of water bath canning. Herein, we'll demystify the process and provide you with a comprehensive, step-by-step guide to mastering water bath canning.

Before we dive into the steps, let's understand the basics of water bath canning. This method is perfect for preserving high-acid foods like fruits, jams, jellies, pickles and tomatoes. The gentle heat of the water bath ensures that your culinary creations are not just safe but also bursting with natural goodness.

Step 1: Gather Your Arsenal

Every successful canning adventure starts with the right tools. So, before you embark on your water bath journey, gather your arsenal:

Jars: Make sure they're free from cracks and defects.

Lids and bands: Ensure they're in pristine condition for a proper seal.

Water bath canner: A large pot with a rack to keep jars off the bottom.

Jar lifter: Trust me, it's a canning game-changer.

Funnel: Keeps your jar rims clean during filling.

Headspace tool: Ensures that perfect amount of space for proper sealing.

Clean towels: For wiping jar rims and preventing slips.

Step 2: Prep Your Ingredients

Ingredients:

Fresh produce: Choose ripe, high-quality fruits or vegetables.

Sweeteners: Sugar, honey, or other sweeteners as per your recipe.

Acids: Lemon juice or vinegar for acidity balance.

Pectin: If your recipe calls for it, for that perfect gel.

Wash, peel, pit, and chop any of your fruits or vegetables according to your recipe. Measure out your sweeteners and acids precisely.

Step 3: Sterilize Your Jars

Cleanliness is next to canning brilliance. Give your jars a good scrub, then sterilize them to create a pristine environment for your culinary creations. You can use your dishwasher or go old-school with boiling water. Once sterilized, keep those jars warm until you're ready to fill them.

Step 4: Heat Things Up

Fill your water bath canner about two-thirds full with enough water to cover your jars by at least an inch. Place it on the stove and start heating. This gives your canner a head start, ensuring it's up to temperature when it's time to process the jars.

Step 5: Fill 'Em Up

With your ingredients prepped and jars warmed, it's showtime! Using your trusty funnel, carefully fill each jar according to your recipe's specifications. Leave the recommended headspace, and use the headspace tool to measure it precisely. An artful filling ensures a masterpiece in every jar.

Step 6: Release the Air Bubbles

No bubbles allowed! Run a non-metallic spatula or bubble remover tool around the inside of each jar to release any trapped air. This step is crucial for achieving a perfect seal and maintaining the integrity of your culinary creations.

Step 7: Seal the Deal

Wipe the rims of your jars with a clean, damp cloth to ensure a proper seal. Place the lid on each jar, followed by the band, and tighten until just fingertip-tight. Now, your jars are ready to take the plunge.

Step 8: Into the Water Bath They Go

Using your jar lifter, carefully place each filled jar onto the rack inside the simmering water bath canner. Ensure the water covers the jars by at least an inch. Now, it's time to let the water work its preserving magic.

Step 9: Bring on the Heat

Once all your jars are snug in the canner, crank up the heat. Bring the water to a gentle, steady boil. Follow your recipe's recommended processing time, and don't forget to adjust for altitude if you're living high in the hills.

Step 10: The Joy of Waiting

As your jars dance in the bubbling water, you might be tempted to sneak a taste, but patience is key. Let the jars process for the designated time. This ensures that harmful microorganisms take their final bow, leaving your jars safe for the pantry stage.

Step 11: Removing and Cooling

With processing complete, it's time for the grand finale. Using your jar lifter, carefully remove each jar and place them on a clean, dry towel. Now, let them cool undisturbed. You might hear the satisfying "ping" of the lids sealing—a glimpse of culinary success.

Step 12: Testing and Storage

After your jars have cooled, perform the "press test" on the center of each lid to ensure a proper seal. If it doesn't give, congratulations! You've just created a jewel. Label your jars with the creation date and store them in a cool, dark place. Now, your pantry is stocked with treasures ready to elevate any meal.

Troubleshooting common issues

Issue 1: The Stubborn Lid - Why Won't It Seal?

Ah, the classic canning woe – the lid that just won't seal. But worry not, my canning comrades. This happens to the best of us. The culprits? It could be residual food on the rim, an uneven jar rim, or not enough headspace. Solution? Wipe the rim clean, check for any nicks, and ensure you've left the recommended headspace. The lid should seal like a charm.

Issue 2: Floating Food - Why Won't It Stay Put?

We've all been there – open a jar, and your peaches are floating like they're in a fruity hot tub. The cause? Air trapped during packing. The fix? Give your jars a good shake before sealing to release those sneaky air bubbles. Pack your ingredients a bit snug next time, and voilà – no more floating surprises.

Issue 3: Siphoning - Why Is My Jar Leaking?

Siphoning, the canner's nemesis. You open your jar, and it looks like a mini flood happened inside. Culprit? Rapid temperature changes during cooling. Solution? Patience is the name of the game. Let your jars cool gradually on a towel, and avoid drafts. This ensures a sealed jar without the drama.

Issue 4: The Great Mystery of the Discolored Product

You open your jar, and instead of vibrant colors, you're met with a slightly off-hue surprise. The culprit? Minerals in hard water can sometimes lead to discoloration. Solution? Use distilled water for your canning adventures, and you'll have picture-perfect preserves every time.

Issue 5: The Case of the Mysterious Cracks

Oh no, a cracked jar – the canner's heartbreak. Culprit? Sudden temperature changes, like moving your hot jars to a cool surface. Solution? Let your jars cool naturally on a towel. If you're dealing with hot-packed goods, preheat your jars to match the food's temperature before filling.

Issue 6: The Runny Jam Dilemma

You pop open a jar of what should be jam, and it's more like a fruity soup. What went wrong? Likely, it's undercooking. Solution? Follow your recipe's processing time to the letter. A good, rolling boil ensures your jam sets up perfectly.

Issue 7: The Sudden Lid Pop - Is My Food Spoiled?

You hear that unexpected "pop" long after canning – panic sets in. Culprit? The lid might not have sealed properly. Solution? Check the seal – press down in the center. If it doesn't give, you're good. If it does, pop it in the fridge and enjoy it soon – it's still safe to eat.

Issue 8: Overcooked Veggies - Why Are They Mushy?

Opening a jar of mushy veggies is like a canning tragedy. The cause? Overcooking during processing. Solution? Adjust your processing time, especially for high-acid foods. A little tweak can make a world of difference.

Issue 9: Unwanted Cloudiness in the Liquid

Your once crystal-clear liquid is now a bit murky. Culprit? Starches in some foods can cloud the liquid. Solution? Blanch starchy foods before canning, and you'll keep that liquid pristine.

Issue 10: The Case of the Lost Labels

You did an amazing job canning, but now your labels are nowhere to be found. The culprit? Moisture during storage can cause labels to peel off. Solution? Invest in water-resistant labels or place a protective layer like clear tape over your labels. Problem solved.

Highlighting the versatility of water bath canning

Water bath canning is your go-to for high-acid foods – think jams, jellies, pickles, and tomatoes. The gentle simmer of the water bath ensures the preservation of these delights without the need for pressure. It's like a gentle hug for your culinary creations, preserving their flavors with a touch of homemade love.

Versatility 1: Jams and Jellies

Ah, the sweet flavor of homemade jams and jellies – the heart and soul of water bath canning. Picture ripe strawberries transformed into a velvety strawberry jam, or the vibrant hues of mixed berries suspended in a delightful jelly. The versatility here lies not just in fruit choices but in flavor combinations. How about a zesty strawberry-basil jam or a spicy peach jalapeño jelly? Water bath canning opens the door to a jam-packed world of creativity.

Versatility 2: Pickles - Crunchy, Tangy, and Beyond

Let's pivot to the crunchy wonders of pickles – a water bath canner's playground. Traditional cucumber pickles are just the beginning. Try your hand at pickling carrots, green beans, or even watermelon rinds. The versatility extends beyond veggies too. How about experimenting with unique spice blends, incorporating dill, garlic, or peppercorns to tailor your pickles to perfection? Water bath canning lets you march to the beat of your own pickling drum.

Versatility 3: Salsas and Relishes

As we continue our water bath canning journey, let's spice things up with salsas and relishes. Fresh tomatoes, peppers, onions – the stage is set for a zesty celebration. Dive into the world of versatility by experimenting with heat levels, adding a pinch of cumin for warmth or a splash of lime for brightness. The result? Customized salsas and relishes that can turn a simple dish into a culinary fiesta.

Versatility 4: Tomatoes Varieties

Tomatoes, the unsung heroes of the kitchen, shine brightly in water bath canning. Move beyond simple tomato sauce and explore the versatility of crushed tomatoes, salsa verde, or even sun-dried tomatoes packed in oil. With water bath canning, you're not just preserving; you're capturing the essence of summer tomatoes to enjoy all year round.

Versatility 5: Fruits - Preserving the Harvest of Nature

The fruity finale of our water bath canning versatility extravaganza brings us to preserved fruits. From peaches and pears to cherries and plums, the options are as diverse as the orchard itself. Infuse your fruits with vanilla, cinnamon, or a hint of citrus for a burst of flavor. Picture a jar of bourbon-infused peaches or vanilla-spiced pears – water bath canning turns your fruit preserves into culinary masterpieces.

Versatility 6: Creative Combinations

Now, let's get adventurous. Water bath canning encourages you to break free from conventional boundaries and blend flavors in ways that surprise and delight the taste buds. Imagine a blueberry-lavender jam or a pineapple-mango salsa – water bath canning isn't just about preservation; it's about crafting edible poetry.

Versatility 7: Beyond the Jar - Culinary Applications

Water bath canning isn't confined to jars alone. Extend its versatility to your daily culinary creations. Use your homemade jams as glazes for meats, stir relishes into dips, or toss pickled veggies into salads. The versatility of water bath canning isn't limited to the preserves; it's a culinary companion that elevates your entire kitchen repertoire.

Elevating Water Bath Techniques

Advanced water bath canning for experienced canners

This is where the seasoned canner transforms into a culinary artist, pushing boundaries, infusing creativity, and mastering techniques that turn each jar into a masterpiece.

Technique 1: Infusing Flavors

In the realm of advanced water bath canning, the infusion of herbs and spices becomes a delicate process. Imagine a peach jam kissed by basil, or a tomato sauce elevated with rosemary and thyme. This technique is about coaxing nuanced flavors from herbs and spices, creating preserves that tell a story with every taste. For experienced canners, it's an opportunity to turn each jar into a canvas for your culinary expression.

Technique 2: Layered Flavors

Advanced canning isn't just about a single note; it's about orchestrating a blend of flavors within one jar. Picture a pickled relish with layers of heat from jalapeños, sweetness from mango, and a hint of smokiness from cumin. This technique involves balancing contrasting elements, creating preserves that tantalize the palate with each bite. For seasoned canners, it's the chance to craft complex, multi dimensional flavor profiles.

Technique 3: Culinary Alchemy

Welcome to the world of advanced water bath canning, where fermentation takes center stage. This technique introduces live cultures, transforming ordinary pickles into probiotic-rich delights. Think beyond cucumbers — ferment carrots, beets, or even green beans. The result? Pickles that not only burst with flavor but also contribute to gut health. For experienced canners, it's the expertise of turning humble veggies into fermented wonders.

Technique 4: Progressive Texture - The Crunch, The Melt, The Burst

Texture becomes an art form in advanced water bath canning. It's about ensuring that each bite is an experience, whether it's the satisfying crunch of a pickled radish or the silky smoothness of a fruit butter. This technique involves meticulous processing times and ingredient choices to achieve the desired mouthfeel. For seasoned canners, it's the mastery of creating preserves that engage the senses with every spoonful.

Technique 5: Creative Mold Breaking

In the advanced canner's repertoire, tradition takes a back seat, and innovation steps to the forefront. Picture pickled strawberries infused with balsamic and black pepper or a savory jam featuring caramelized onions and thyme. This technique is about breaking free from the expected, experimenting with unconventional pairings that redefine the boundaries of preserves. For experienced canners, it's an invitation to unleash your creativity and surprise your taste buds.

Technique 6: Culinary Harmonization

Now, let's embark on a journey around the world without leaving your kitchen. Advanced water bath canning allows you to infuse global flavors into your preserves. Think of a mango chutney inspired by Indian spices or a salsa verde that captures the essence of Mexican cuisine. This technique involves understanding the nuances of international spices and techniques, creating jars that reflect a world of culinary influences. For seasoned canners, it's a passport to global gastronomy within the confines of your pantry.

Infusing flavors through creative recipes

The foundation of creative flavor infusion lies in your choice of ingredients. Imagine the sweet, floral notes of lavender shining with the tartness of blueberries or the warmth of ginger embracing the earthiness of peaches. As a canner with experience, you have the freedom to play with a diverse palette of flavors. Fresh herbs, spices, and unexpected twists – they're your secret weapons for creating preserves that tell a story with every spoonful.

Now, let's dive into the heart of the matter – the technique of infusing flavors. It's not just about adding ingredients; it's about coaxing out their essence and letting them intertwine in a show of flavors. Picture this: a tomato jam elevated with balsamic, basil, and a hint of chili heat or a citrus-infused strawberry preserve that sings with brightness. For experienced canners, this technique is your chance to be a flavor maestro, composing jars that resonate with complexity.

Beyond the sweetness of traditional jams, advanced canning opens the door to savory infusions that redefine the boundaries of preserves. Picture a caramelized onion and rosemary jam that transforms a simple cracker into a culinary delight or a roasted red pepper and thyme relish that elevates grilled meats to new heights. The world of savory infusions is vast, and as a seasoned canner, you have the skill to explore its every corner.

For those who appreciate the influence of sweet and heat, advanced water bath canning provides the perfect stage. Infuse your preserves with the smoky warmth of chipotle peppers or the fiery kick of jalapeños. Imagine a mango habanero salsa that adds a burst of excitement to your dishes or a peach and sriracha chutney that keeps your taste buds on their toes. Sweet and heat, a duet made in canning heaven.

One of the joys of creative flavor infusion is the ability to draw inspiration from cuisines around the world. As a seasoned canner, you can transform your kitchen into a global culinary adventure. Imagine a Moroccan-inspired apricot preserve with hints of cinnamon and cumin or a Thai basil and coconut-infused pineapple jam that transports you to tropical shores. Your jars become passports to international flavor destinations.

While we celebrate creativity, let's not forget the science of balance. Experienced canners understand that the interplay of sweet, sour, salty, bitter, and umami is the key to a well-balanced infusion. It's not just about adding ingredients; it's about knowing how to harmonize them. Balancing flavors is your superpower, ensuring that each jar is a symphony, not a cacophony.

In the world of creative flavor infusion, there are no strict rules – only guidelines waiting to be bent or broken. As a canner with experience, you have the freedom to experiment fearlessly. Don't be afraid to push the boundaries, try unexpected combinations, and let your taste buds guide you. Maybe a lavender-infused peach compote or a blackberry and sage jam – the possibilities are as endless as your creativity.

Advanced Pickling Techniques

Introducing fermentation as a pickling method

Fermentation, in the context of pickling, involves the natural process where beneficial bacteria (lactic acid bacteria) work their magic on vegetables, breaking down sugars into lactic acid. This not only imparts that distinctive tangy flavor but also acts as a natural preservative, keeping your pickles crisp and vibrant.

As we step into the world of fermented pickles, the choice of vegetables becomes crucial. Cucumbers are the classic stars, but don't shy away from experimenting with carrots, radishes, or even cauliflower. The key is to opt for fresh, crisp produce – the kind that eagerly soaks up the flavors of fermentation.

In the world of fermentation, the brine is your secret weapon. It's a simple concoction of water and salt that creates the perfect environment for those friendly bacteria to thrive. The salt not only seasons your pickles but also acts as a natural barrier against undesirable microbes. It's a delicate balance, and as a seasoned canner, you have the finesse to get it just right. Unlike quick pickles, fermented pickles are patient beings. They revel in time – days, weeks, or even months. As a canner with experience, you understand that the magic of fermentation unfolds slowly. It's about allowing the flavors to develop, letting the tanginess deepen, and savoring the anticipation of what's to come.

One of the joys of fermentation is the versatility it brings to your pickle palate. As a seasoned canner, you can play with a myriad of flavors. Imagine garlic and dill-infused cucumber pickles or beet and ginger-tinged kraut. Fermentation allows you to infuse your pickles with creative combinations that go beyond the ordinary. Nevertheless, every fermenting adventure comes with its quirks, and as an experienced canner, you're equipped to troubleshoot. Worried about a cloudy brine? Concerned about an unexpected fizz? Fear not! We'll look into common fermentation hiccups and how to steer your pickling ship back on course.

Fermented pickles aren't just about flavor; they're also about embracing the goodness of probiotics. As you munch on these tangy delights, you're introducing beneficial bacteria to your gut, promoting a happy and healthy digestive system. It's a win-win – delicious pickles and a boost to your well-being.

Exploring pickling beyond cucumbers, including fruits and unconventional vegetables

As a passionate canner, you know the drill – cucumbers, jars, and the presence of brine. But what if I told you the pickling world was vast, and the time has come to shatter the cucumber mold? It's a culinary revolution, my friends, where fruits and unconventional vegetables become the center for our pickling artistry

Envision this: pickled strawberries combined with balsamic, watermelon rinds infused with minty freshness, or mango slices transformed into tangy delights. The world of pickling extends its arms to embrace the sweetness of fruits, creating a spectrum of flavors that challenges the traditional notion of what a pickle can be. As a seasoned canner, be ready to balance the sweetness with the tang, turning each jar into a burst of unexpected delight.

It's time to think beyond the usual suspects lining your produce aisle. Beets, radishes, and even Brussels sprouts – these unconventional veggies are the rebels of the pickling world. Imagine a medley of pickled beets with cumin and coriander, or radishes pickled in a fiery sriracha brine. As a canner with experience, you understand that these unconventional choices add a layer of excitement to your pickling repertoire.

In our pickling sojourn, flavor becomes the brushstroke on our culinary fabric. Fruits and unconventional vegetables are not just ingredients; they're the colors that paint a masterpiece. A peach and jalapeño relish, a blueberry and basil chutney, or a pickled fennel and orange salad – the pickling palette is as diverse as your creativity allows. It's about crafting combinations that not only tickle the taste buds but also challenge your notion of what belongs in a pickle jar.

As we explore pickling beyond cucumbers, the art of balance takes center stage. Sweet fruits meet tangy brines, and unconventional veggies challenge our taste buds with bold flavors. It's a delicate combination, balancing act that seasoned canners like you approach with finesse. The sweet, the tangy, the bold – each element finds its place in the pickling tapestry you're weaving.

There's a magic that happens when fruits and unconventional vegetables meet the pickling jar. The sweetness intensifies, the tanginess deepens, and the flavors meld into a shade of taste. Pickled peaches become a revelation on your cheese board, while Brussels sprouts take on a new life as a zesty sidekick to your sandwiches. As an experienced canner, you're not just preserving; you're creating unexpected culinary magic.

Troubleshooting tips for common pickling challenges

The pickling journey – a thrilling ride that sometimes encounters bumps along the way. As a dedicated canner, you've likely faced a few hiccups: cloudy brine, limp pickles, unexpected fizz. Don't panic! We're here to unravel the mysteries and equip you with the troubleshooting savvy needed to conquer common pickling challenges.

Troubleshooting Challenge #1: Cloudy Brine Conundrum

You open your jar of pickles, and the brine looks more like a mysterious fog than a clear solution. What went wrong? Cloudy brine is often the result of minerals in the water or additives in the salt. The fix? Use distilled water and high-quality salt without anti-caking agents. Your brine will be crystal clear, setting the stage for pickle perfection.

Troubleshooting Challenge #2: The Lament of Limp Pickles

It's a pickle lover's lament – instead of crisp and crunchy, your pickles are a tad limp. Where did that crunch go? The culprit is often an inadequate cucumber soak before pickling. Ensure your cucumbers take a relaxing bath in an ice-cold water soak before they meet the brine. This ensures they absorb the flavors without sacrificing their crispness. Limp pickles, be gone!

Troubleshooting Challenge #3: Unexpected Fizz Fiasco

You open a jar, and instead of the satisfying "pop," you're met with an unexpected fizz. What in the pickling world is happening? Don't fret, it's likely just the result of continued fermentation in the jar. The solution? Give your pickles an extra day or two in the fridge before enjoying them. That fizz might just be the sign of a lively, probiotic-rich batch.

Troubleshooting Challenge #4: The Perils of Pickle Floaters

Floating pickles – a sight no canner wants to see. If your pickles are defying gravity, it's a sign of insufficient packing. Pack those jars tight, ensuring the cucumbers are snug and cozy. This not only prevents floaters but also maximizes the flavor infusion. Remember, a well-packed jar is a happy jar!

Troubleshooting Challenge #5: The Color Conundrum

You envisioned vibrant, jewel-toned pickles, but instead, you're faced with a faded reality. What gives? The color conundrum often arises when using iodized salt, which can dull the hues of your pickles. Opt for non-iodized salt, and your pickles will boast the brilliant colors you've been dreaming of.

Troubleshooting Challenge #6: The Too-Salty Surprise

Ah, the perils of over-enthusiastic salting – your pickles are saltier than the Dead Sea. Don't panic, this happens to the best of us. The remedy is simple: balance. Increase the water content in your brine, diluting the saltiness without compromising flavor. Your taste buds will thank you.

Troubleshooting Challenge #7: The Mystery of Mold

You open a jar, and there it is – a fuzzy visitor on your pickles. Mold has made an unwelcome appearance. The likely culprit? Insufficient headspace or improper cleaning of the jar rims. Ensure a generous headspace, and meticulously clean those rims before sealing. Mold, meet your match!

Troubleshooting Challenge #8: The Shrinking Pickle Dilemma

Your pickles were plump and promising, but post-canning, they've taken on a shrinking act. The culprit here is often under-processing. Ensure your pickles receive adequate processing time, allowing them to maintain their size and shape post-jarring. A little extra time in the canner is a small price for plump perfection.

Pickling for Health

The potential health benefits of consuming pickled food

You might be accustomed to viewing pickles as mere accompaniments to sandwiches or cheese boards, but what if I told you they carry a hidden treasure trove of health benefits? It's true – beyond the crunch and tang, pickled foods offer a spectrum of wellness perks that might just elevate them to the status of a culinary superfood.

At the heart of pickled wellness lies the magic of probiotics. Fermented pickles are teeming with these friendly bacteria that promote a flourishing gut microbiome. As you relish those tangy bites, you're inviting a battalion of beneficial microorganisms into your digestive system. A happy gut translates to improved digestion, better nutrient absorption, and a strengthened immune system. Who knew a jar of pickles could be the unsung hero of your gut health?

Fermentation, the enchanting process behind pickling, doesn't just add a burst of flavor — it unlocks the nutritional potential of your ingredients. During this transformative journey, certain compounds in the vegetables break down, making essential nutrients more bioavailable. Think of it as a culinary prowess that turns ordinary veggies into nutrient-rich powerhouses. With each pickle you enjoy, you're savoring a bite-sized nutritional boost.

In the pursuit of wellness, calorie-conscious snacking often becomes a priority. Here's where pickles shine as a guilt-free delight. With minimal calories and a satisfying crunch, they make for a wholesome snack that won't tip the scales. Swap out those calorie-laden munchies for a jar of pickles, and you'll find yourself satisfying cravings without compromising your wellness goals. In the same vein, staying hydrated is a cornerstone of well-being, and pickles offer a unique way to contribute to your daily fluid intake. The brine, a concoction of water, salt, and spices, not only infuses your pickles with flavor but also serves as a hydrating elixir. It's a tasty alternative to plain water, especially for those who find sipping H_2O a tad mundane.

After a workout or on a scorching day, your body craves electrolytes to stay balanced. Enter pickles, a natural source of replenishing minerals like sodium, potassium, and magnesium found in the brine. Forget the artificial sports drinks; reach for a pickle instead to keep your electrolytes in check and support overall hydration.

Surprisingly, the vinegar in pickled foods may play a role in managing blood sugar levels. Some studies suggest that vinegar consumption, a key component in many pickling recipes, could contribute to improved insulin sensitivity, aiding in glucose regulation. While not a substitute for medical advice, it adds another layer to the potential health benefits of enjoying pickled foods.

Wellness isn't just about nutrients; it's also about mindful eating. Pickles, with their bold flavors and satisfying crunch, bring a sensory delight to your plate. The act of savoring each bite promotes mindful munching, helping you appreciate the textures and tastes that unfold with every nibble. It's a holistic approach to wellness that extends beyond the nutritional content.

As you weave the potential health benefits of pickled foods into your wellness drapery, consider creative ways to incorporate them into your daily routine. Top your salads with pickled beets, enjoy fermented pickles as a side dish, or elevate your sandwich with the zing of pickled onions. The key is to savor these delights intentionally, recognizing the wellness boost they bring to your culinary repertoire.

Introducing probiotics and their role in fermented pickling

Imagine your jar of fermenting pickles as a bustling party for the tiniest of guests – probiotics. These good bacteria are the life of the pickling party, and their role goes beyond simply flavoring your veggies. They're your gut's best pals, and as you savor those tangy bites, you're treating your digestive system to a microbial fiesta.

Let's start with the basics. Probiotics are like the rockstars of the microbial world. They are live microorganisms, the good guys, that bring health benefits to your gut. You might not see them, but trust me, they're working their magic with every passing moment your pickles spend in that jar.

So, how do these probiotics end up in your pickles? It's all about fermentation. As your veggies soak in a salty brine, a magical transformation happens. The probiotics, like *Lactobacillus* and its buddies, flourish in this environment, turning sugars into lactic acid. This not only gives your pickles their signature tang but also creates a fortress against harmful bacteria.

Here's the real charm of probiotics – they are your gut's guardian angels. When you consume these friendly bacteria through fermented pickles, it's like sending reinforcements to your digestive army. They promote a happy, diverse microbiome, which is the secret sauce for top-notch digestion, nutrient absorption, and a robust immune system. Your gut is like a lively orchestra, and probiotics play a crucial role in maintaining its harmony. By introducing probiotics through fermented pickles, you're contributing to the biodiversity of your gut microbiome. A diverse microbiome isn't just a fancy term; it's linked to overall well-being and a digestive system that hums along happily.

Sure, probiotics are MVPs for your gut, but their benefits don't stop there. Recent studies hint at a connection between a flourishing gut microbiome – thanks to probiotics – and a resilient immune system. So, every time you relish a fermented pickle, you're not just treating your taste buds; you're giving your immune system a potential boost.

As you embark on your probiotic-rich pickling adventure, consider these tips to make the most of the microbial goodness:

1. Fresh and Organic: Start with quality veggies for a robust microbial population. Go for fresh and organic whenever possible.
2. Let Nature Work: Embrace natural fermentation. Avoid shortcuts like vinegar or additives that might hinder the growth of good bacteria.
3. Patience is Key: Don't rush the process. The longer the fermentation, the more probiotic punch your pickles pack.
4. Mix It Up: Experiment with various veggies, herbs, and spices. Different ingredients bring different strains of probiotics to the party.

5. Chill Out: Once your pickles reach the desired tanginess, pop them in the fridge. It slows down fermentation and preserves those precious probiotics.

The nutritional value of various pickled items

As you pop open a jar of your homemade pickles, have you ever wondered about the nutritional riches concealed within? It's not just about the crunch and the tang; it's about infusing your body with an array of vitamins, minerals, and beneficial compounds. Let's unravel the nutritional value of various pickled items and discover why your pickling passion is a culinary and health win.

Your pickles are more than just a zesty sidekick to your meals; they're a potent source of essential vitamins and minerals. From vitamin C to manganese, pickled items bring a spectrum of nutrients to your plate. These micronutrients play crucial roles in immune function, bone health, and overall vitality.

As we explored in the previous chapters, fermented pickles are a playground for probiotics. These friendly bacteria not only add a delightful tang to your pickles but also contribute to a flourishing gut microbiome. A healthy gut isn't just about digestion; it's linked to improved mood, immune support, and even weight management.

Now, let's address the pickle in the room – sodium. Yes, pickled items do contain salt, a key player in the pickling process. While it's essential for preservation and flavor, it's wise to be mindful of your sodium intake. Enjoy your pickles as part of a balanced diet, and consider low-sodium alternatives if sodium intake is a concern.

Fiber often takes the back seat in discussions about pickled items, but it's a silent hero in your jar. The vegetables that soak up the pickling brine become not only crunchy delights but also carriers of dietary fiber. Fiber supports digestive health, helps manage cholesterol levels, and contributes to a feeling of fullness.

Don't underestimate the power of antioxidants lurking in your pickled treats. The colorful array of vegetables, herbs, and spices in your jars is a visual cue to the diverse antioxidants within. These compounds combat free radicals, offering potential protection against oxidative stress and inflammation.

Craving a snack? Your jar of pickles might just be the answer. Instead of reaching for processed snacks, consider the nutritional perks of pickled items. They're low in calories, high in flavor, and bring a satisfying crunch – a smart choice for those aiming for a wholesome snacking experience.

As you assemble your pickler's plate – a medley of pickled vegetables, fruits, and perhaps even meats – you're not just creating a palate-pleasing dish; you're crafting a choice of nutrition. The combination of vitamins, minerals, probiotics, and antioxidants in your pickled spread contributes to a well-rounded and nourishing culinary experience.

Chapter 7

Pressure Canning Mastery

Demystifying Pressure Canning

Selecting appropriate foods for pressure canning

Before we jump into the selection process, let's revisit the essence of pressure canning. It's the hero of the low-acid preservation world, saving the day when you're dealing with ingredients like vegetables, meats, and legumes. The pressure canner, our trusty director, orchestrates a performance where high pressure and temperature join forces to guarantee a safe and delicious finale.

Vegetables, the leading lady of the pressure canning show, offer a vibrant and nutritious performance. From the crispness of green beans to the earthy notes of carrots, pressure canning ensures these veggies retain their texture, flavor, and nutritional value. Think of your favorite veggies, and chances are, they're ready for their close-up in the pressure canning pantheon.

Now, let's talk about the essential co-stars – proteins and legumes. Meats, poultry, and beans join the ensemble, adding a protein-packed punch to your pressure-canned creations. Imagine the convenience of having ready-to-use beans or a jar of savory chicken for quick and hearty meals. Pressure canning elevates these ingredients into culinary co-stars that steal the spotlight.

Pressure canning extends its repertoire to include supporting roles like soups, stews, and sauces. Picture a busy evening when you can simply open a jar of homemade tomato sauce or hearty beef stew. Pressure canning allows you to preserve the richness and depth of these dishes, ensuring they're ready to take the stage whenever you need them.

Now, let's get practical about selecting the right foods for pressure canning success. It's like holding auditions – each ingredient has its unique qualities, and you want to make sure they complement each other for a harmonious flavor.

Just like a movie director seeks top-notch actors, you want the freshest produce and meats for your pressure canning endeavors. Opt for ingredients at their peak to guarantee a show stopping performance in every jar. Consider the flavor profile of your ingredients. Combining a variety of veggies, proteins, and legumes not only enhances taste but also ensures a well-rounded nutritional offering. Think of it as crafting a culinary ensemble that hits all the right notes.

Texture is crucial in the world of pressure canning. While some ingredients, like potatoes, might soften during the process, others, like beans, retain a pleasant firmness. The key is to curate a cast that complements each other in terms of texture, creating a delightful palate experience. Just as movies capture the essence of a season, let your pressure canning reflect the rhythm of nature. Choose ingredients that are in season for the freshest and most flavorful results. It's like capturing the essence of summer in a jar of succulent tomatoes or the warmth of autumn in a medley of root vegetables.

As we wrap up our journey through the pressure canning panorama, remember that safety is the curtain call that can't be missed. Always follow USDA guidelines, adhere to recommended processing times, and ensure your pressure canner is in top-notch condition. Safety is the backbone of every successful pressure canning performance.

Step-by-step instructions for safe and effective pressure canning

The first step is assembling the cast – your ingredients. Think of this as the casting call for your pressure canner drama. Choose the freshest vegetables, meats, or legumes that showcase their peak flavors. Like selecting actors, quality matters for a stellar performance in every jar. Now, let's select the appropriate foods, the script for our canning play. Vegetables, meats, and legumes are the protagonists here, ready to deliver a culinary brilliance. Ensure a balanced cast for a harmonious flavor combination in your jars. Think of it as creating a culinary ensemble that dances on your taste buds.

Every good play has a script, and for pressure canning, the USDA guidelines take center stage. They are the backbone of a safe and effective canning performance. Familiarize yourself with these guidelines, as they ensure your production meets the highest safety standards. Safety is our top priority on this culinary stage.

Now, let's shift our focus to the behind-the-scenes action – preparing your equipment. Just as actors get ready for their roles, your pressure canner and jars need to be prepped for the main event. Your pressure canner is the leading actor, and it needs to be in top-notch condition. Check for any wear and tear, ensuring the sealing ring and vent pipe are functioning perfectly. Think of it as your leading actor hitting the gym for peak performance. At the same time, inspect your jars – the supporting cast – for any cracks or defects. They need to be in perfect condition to complement the leading actor. Sterilize them thoroughly, setting the stage for a flawless canning performance.

Now, it's time for the main event – the step-by-step instructions for safe and effective pressure canning.

Step 1: Preheat the Pressure Canner

Just as the lights dim before a play, preheat your pressure canner. Add a few inches of hot water to create a steamy atmosphere for the canning action.

Step 2: Load Your Jars

Place your prepared jars filled with culinary goodness into the preheated pressure canner. It's like actors taking their positions on the stage.

Step 3: Secure the Lid

Like the curtain rising on a play, secure the lid of your pressure canner. Ensure it's tightly sealed, ready to capture the magic inside.

Step 4: Vent the Canner

Release any trapped air by allowing steam to escape for 10 minutes. It's the pressure canner's way of taking a deep breath before the performance.

Step 5: Reach the Desired Pressure

Gradually increase the heat until you reach the recommended pressure. This is where the culinary expertise happens – high pressure and temperature working together for a safe canning masterpiece.

Step 6: Processing Time

Now, let the canning play unfold by maintaining the pressure for the recommended processing time. It's the duration your ingredients need to reach their preserved perfection.

Step 7: Cooling Down

Once the processing time is over, turn off the heat and let the pressure canner cool down naturally. It's the grand finale, where your jars have completed their canning performance.

Curtain Call: Safety First, Applause Later

As the curtain falls on our pressure canning play, remember that safety is the applause at the end. Allow the pressure canner to cool completely before removing the lid. Your safe and effective canning production is now ready for an encore in your pantry.

Exploring the benefits of pressure canning

The first benefit that takes center stage is the ability to preserve the essence of your ingredients. Pressure canning operates like a culinary time capsule, locking in the freshness, nutrients, and vibrant flavors that make your produce unique. Imagine savoring the peak taste of summer tomatoes or the hearty richness of autumnal root vegetables, all year round.

Pressure canning isn't just about preserving; it's about expanding your culinary repertoire. Imagine having the power to can a variety of low-acid foods – from savory stews to hearty legumes. It's the versatility that pressure canning brings to your kitchen, allowing you to go beyond the basics and explore a rich diverse of flavors and textures.

Let's not forget to shine a spotlight on the paramount importance of safety. Pressure canning acts as your kitchen's guardian, eliminating the risk of harmful microorganisms that could spoil your culinary products. It's your ticket to confident and safe home canning, ensuring every jar on your shelf is a masterpiece of security and taste.

Pressure canning dispels the myths and fears that may have held you back. Worried about botulism? Fear not! As we dissect the benefits, you'll find that following USDA guidelines and adhering to safe practices create an impenetrable shield against any canning anxieties. It operates on a faster timeline than traditional water bath methods. In the time it takes for a water bath canner to waltz, a pressure canner sprints to the finish line. It's the canning method for those who relish efficiency without compromising on flavor.

Overcoming common fears and misconceptions

1. Fear: "It's Too Complicated!"

Reality Check: Panic not, my fellow canner! While pressure canning may seem intricate, today's canners are designed for simplicity. Follow a reliable recipe, stick to safety guidelines, and you'll find yourself sailing smoothly through the process.

2. Fear: "Will My Jars Explode?"

Reality Check: The explosive myth! When done correctly, pressure canning is a safe method endorsed by food safety experts. Trust your canner, maintain proper pressure, and stick to recommended processing times. Your jars are more likely to burst from excitement for the culinary wonders inside than from pressure canning.

3. Fear: "Loss of Flavor and Texture"

Reality Check: Quite the opposite! Pressure canning intensifies flavors and maintains the texture of your ingredients. Say goodbye to mushy vegetables and hello to jars bursting with the essence of freshness. Your taste buds are in for a delightful surprise!

4. Fear: "I'll Poison My Loved Ones!"

Reality Check: Safety first, canners! By following USDA-approved guidelines, using reliable recipes, and maintaining proper equipment, you're steering clear of any food safety hazards. Pressure canning is your ally in preserving food while keeping harmful microorganisms at bay.

5. Fear: "It's Only for Experts!"

Reality Check: Nonsense! While pressure canning may seem intimidating initially, consider it a culinary adventure waiting to unfold. With the right information and a dash of courage, you'll soon find yourself confidently navigating the canning waters, no expert title required.

6. Fear: "I Don't Have Time for This!"

Reality Check: Time-efficient canning ahoy! Pressure canning is a culinary time-saver. With reduced cooking times, you're not only preserving flavors but also reclaiming precious moments in your day. Picture a pantry stocked with delicious time-saving treasures.

7. Misconception: "It Alters the Taste"

Reality Check: Brace yourself for flavor elevation! Pressure canning doesn't alter taste; it enhances it. Expect vibrant, flavorful creations that capture the essence of each ingredient. It's not just about preservation; it's about savoring the best of every jar.

8. Misconception: "You Need Special Ingredients"

Reality Check: Raid your pantry and market with confidence! Pressure canning celebrates the beauty of everyday ingredients. There's no need for exotic finds; it's about preserving what you love and what's readily available, ensuring your jars reflect your unique culinary preferences.

9. Misconception: "It's Only for Large Batches"

Reality Check: Size-flexible canning at your service! Pressure canning adapts to your needs. Whether you're preserving a bounty or crafting small batches, your canner is your culinary companion. Say farewell to food waste and hello to a pantry tailored to your preferences.

10. Misconception: "It's Not Worth the Effort"

Reality Check: Effort that pays delicious dividends! The joy of opening a jar filled with your own culinary creation is unparalleled. Pressure canning isn't just about preservation; it's about savoring the fruits of your labor. The effort is a small investment for a pantry brimming with treasures.

Safety measures and precautions

The following safety and precautions should be strictly adhered to:

1. Canner Check: Before you set sail, ensure your pressure canner is in shipshape condition. Check for any signs of wear, including seals, gauges, and vent pipes. A well-maintained canner is your steadfast companion in the canning seas.

2. Follow the Captain's Orders (AKA Your Recipe): Every culinary adventure needs a map. In canning, it's your trusted recipe. Follow it to the letter. Altering ingredients or processing times can steer you into uncharted and potentially unsafe waters.

3. Seal the Deal: Jar seals are your first mates in preservation. Ensure they are flawless before, during, and after processing. A compromised seal can lead to spoilage or, in extreme cases, foodborne illnesses.

4. Mind the Altitude: The altitude is your navigational challenge. Adjust processing times according to your location. The higher you go, the longer the processing time needed. Charts and guidelines are your treasure maps in this altitude adventure.

5. Heed the Pressure: Your pressure gauge is your navigational compass. Maintain the pressure as directed by your recipe. Too low, and you risk under-processing; too high, and you might compromise the quality of your goods.

6. Jars' Dive into Hot Waters: Before your jars embark on their hot bath, ensure they're properly preheated. Placing cold food in hot jars can lead to thermal shock and, in the worst-case scenario, cracked jars.

7. Respect the Vent: Allow your canner to vent steam for a full ten minutes before pressurizing. This prelude ensures any air pockets are expelled, leaving you with jars ready for a safe and sealed voyage.

8. Lid's Tale of Tightening: Tighten jar lids with the precision of a seasoned sailor, but don't overdo it. Fingertip tight is the motto – firm enough to seal but not so tight that your jars become pressurized landmines.

9. Cooling Calmly: Once the processing is complete, resist the urge to rush the cooling process. Let your jars cool naturally and gradually. Placing hot jars in a cold breeze might shatter your hard-earned creations.

10. Inspection Is Key: Before stowing your jars in the treasure trove (your pantry), inspect each one. Look for any signs of spoilage, leaks, or compromised seals. A thorough inspection ensures only the finest treasures make it to the shelf.

11. Label, Label, Label: As you stow away your canned treasures, label each jar with the date and content. This practice not only helps you keep track but also ensures you consume your bounty at its peak.

12. Landlubber's Rule: When in Doubt, Throw It Out

If, during your inspection, you encounter any doubts about the safety of your canned goods, don't hesitate. Discard them. Your safety at sea (and in the kitchen) is paramount.

Preserving Soups, Stews, and More

The versatility of pressure canning for preserving liquid-based recipes

In this section, we will be unfurling the sails of versatility and navigate the liquid-based seas of home canning. Get ready to infuse your pantry with the essence of savory broths, luscious soups, and more.

1. Broth Brilliance: The first mate in our liquid-based journey is the almighty broth. Whether it's a rich chicken broth or a hearty vegetable stock, pressure canning allows you to capture the essence of your culinary creations. Imagine the convenience of a ready-to-pour broth for your soups, stews, and risottos.

2. Soup's On – Anytime: Picture this: a chilly evening, a craving for comforting soup, and your homemade creation ready in minutes. With pressure canning, you can preserve your favorite soups – from classic tomato bisque to exotic ramen broths. Say goodbye to canned soups with mysterious ingredients and hello to your wholesome concoctions.

3. Stew for the Win: A simmering stew bubbling on the stove is a sight to behold. But what if you could capture that magic in a jar? Pressure canning turns this dream into reality. Beef stew, chili, or ratatouille – your favorite stews can be preserved and ready to dazzle your taste buds at a moment's notice.

4. Saucy Solutions: From marinara to curry sauces, pressure canning extends its versatility to liquid-based sauces. Seal the flavors of your homemade creations, allowing you to whip up gourmet meals in a fraction of the time. Weeknight dinners will never be the same.

5. Tantalizing Tomatoes: The versatility of pressure canning shines with tomatoes. Capture the vibrancy of summer by canning your tomato puree, sauce, or salsa. Enjoy the taste of sun-ripened tomatoes in your dishes all year round.

6. The Sweet Side – Fruit Compotes: Who said pressure canning is only for savory delights? Explore the sweet side of liquid preservation with fruit compotes. Imagine the joy of a dollop of your homemade apple compote gracing your morning pancakes. With pressure canning, breakfast gets a flavorful upgrade.

Sharing innovative recipes for soups, stews, and sauces

Soups That Warm the Soul

1. Creamy Tomato Basil Bliss: Let's kick off our liquid feast with a classic – creamy tomato basil soup. Imagine the rich, velvety texture and the burst of tomato and basil flavors in every spoonful. Pressure canning allows you to capture this comfort in a jar, ready to be heated and savored on the coldest of days.

2. Chicken Noodle Euphoria: Beat the winter blues with the timeless delight of chicken noodle soup. Load your jars with succulent chicken, hearty noodles, and a medley of vegetables. With pressure canning, a steaming bowl of this classic is just a jar away.

3. Harvest Minestrone Magic: Embrace the bounty of the harvest with a minestrone that packs a flavorful punch. Beans, veggies, and pasta dance together in a harmony of taste. Pressure canning locks in the vibrant flavors, making every jar a celebration of seasonal goodness.

Stews to Satisfy

1. Beef Bourguignon Brilliance: Elevate your culinary prowess with the luxurious flavors of beef bourguignon. Tender beef, red wine, and a melody of vegetables – pressure canning transforms this gourmet delight into a convenient showpiece. A taste of France in your own pantry.

2. Vegetarian Chili Fiesta: For the spice lovers, a vegetarian chili that's a fiesta of flavors. Beans, peppers, and a zesty tomato base – canned to perfection. Enjoy the convenience of having a spicy kick whenever the craving strikes.

3. Lamb and Lentil Extravaganza: Dare to be different with a lamb and lentil stew that's a feast for the senses. Pressure canning captures the essence of lamb, lentils, and aromatic spices. An exotic journey in a jar.

Saucy Sensations

1. Mushroom Alfredo Marvel: Dive into decadence with a mushroom alfredo sauce that transforms any pasta into a gourmet experience. Pressure canning preserves the creamy texture and umami goodness, making every pasta night a celebration.

2. Bold and Spicy Salsa Verde: Kick up the heat with a salsa verde that's as versatile as it is flavorful. Whether as a sauce for tacos or a dip for chips, pressure canning ensures a constant supply of bold and spicy goodness.

3. Homemade Marinara Masterpiece: Bid farewell to store-bought marinara with a homemade masterpiece. Tomatoes, garlic, and herbs meld into a sauce that elevates pizzas, pastas, and more. Pressure canning – your shortcut to gourmet Italian nights.

Navigating the Liquid Canning Seas

1. Jar Jargon: Equip yourself with wide-mouthed jars for easy filling. Opt for jars with impeccable seals to ensure the freshness of your liquid creations.

2. Headroom Hues: Leave the right headspace to avoid spills during the canning process. A little extra space goes a long way in ensuring a pristine seal.

3. Flavorful Finale: Enhance your liquid creations with a pinch of salt, herbs, or spices. Experimentation is the key to finding your signature blend.

4. Temperature Tango: Follow recommended processing times and pressure levels for safe and flavorful results. The perfect tango between time and pressure is the secret to a well-preserved creation.

5. Label Like a Pro: Maintain an organized pantry by labeling your jars with content and date. A well-labeled pantry is a treasure trove of culinary possibilities.

Storage tips for canned liquid goods

Before we dive into storage specifics, allow your liquid creations a moment to cool post-canning. This is not only a safety measure but also a practice that enhances the longevity of flavors.

1. Start with the basics – labeling. Your jars are like musical notes, and labeling them properly is akin to creating sheet music. Include the date of canning and the contents to orchestrate a harmonious storage system.

2. Layered Storage: When it comes to soups, consider storing them in layers. Heavier ingredients tend to settle at the bottom over time. Give your jars a gentle shake before opening to distribute flavors evenly.

3. Refrigeration Advantage: While most canned soups can rest in your pantry, a stint in the refrigerator for a few days before transferring to the pantry can enhance their freshness.

It's like giving your soup a VIP lounge experience before it takes center stage on your dinner table.

4. Rotation Rhythms: Practice the art of rotation. As new batches join your pantry, shift the older ones to the front. This ensures that your liquid collections maintain a vibrant and well-balanced melody.

5. Choosing the Right Spot: Store your canned stews in a cool, dark place. Exposing them to direct sunlight can lead to a gradual decline in flavor quality. Think of it as protecting your stew's backstage pass from the harsh spotlight.

6. Regular Inventory Checks: Just like a maestro knows their orchestra, stay attuned to your pantry inventory. Regularly check for any signs of compromised seals or visual changes in your stews. This way, you can quickly replace any jar that's not in tune with your standards.

7. Mind the Headspace: Sauces, being more fluid, may require a bit more attention to headspace. Ensure you leave the recommended amount of space between the sauce and the lid. This helps maintain the seal integrity and prevents messy leaks.

8. Chilling for Preservation: Some sauces, especially those with higher acidity, benefit from chilling in the refrigerator for a brief period after canning. This short stay enhances their flavors and preserves their vibrant color.

9. Avoid Extremes: While your pantry may be a suitable home for most canned goods, avoid extreme temperatures. Excessive heat can compromise seals, while freezing may alter the texture of your liquid creations.

10. Strategic Shelf Placement: Arrange your jars strategically on shelves. Stacking them neatly reduces the chances of accidental bumps or jars getting lost in the back, ensuring each one gets its time in the spotlight.

11. Plan for Visibility: Design your pantry like a well-organized library. Group similar items together, ensuring that when you're seeking a specific soup or sauce, you can easily spot it in your well-arranged collection.

Creative ideas for pressure canning meats, soups, and more

Pressure canning is the turning of ordinary ingredients into extraordinary, shelf-stable delights. Let's explore creative ways to utilize this technique and elevate your culinary repertoire.

1. Embrace the flexibility of pressure canning by creating versatile meat medleys. Combine chicken, beef, or pork with a melody of herbs, spices, and broths for ready-to-use protein that can star in various dishes.

2. Elevate your soups, stews, and sauces by pressure canning flavorful meat broths. These liquid gold jars add depth and richness to any recipe, saving you precious time during busy cooking sessions.

3. Transform tough cuts into succulent, shredded wonders. Pressure canning renders meats fork-tender, ready to be effortlessly incorporated into tacos, sandwiches, or hearty casseroles.

4. Capture the essence of each season by pressure canning soups made from fresh, seasonal ingredients. From a vibrant summer gazpacho to a robust winter minestrone, your pantry can become a soup lover's paradise.

5. Craft one-jar wonders by pressure canning complete soups. Imagine opening a jar to find a perfectly balanced meal, rich with vegetables, proteins, and aromatic spices – an instant and satisfying feast.

6. Embark on a global soup adventure by experimenting with international flavors. Pressure canning allows you to savor the warmth of a Thai coconut soup, the tang of a Mexican pozole, or the comfort of an Italian wedding soup anytime you desire.

7. Extend your pressure canning prowess to grains. Prepare jars of perfectly cooked rice, quinoa, or pasta, ready to serve as a hearty base for your culinary creations.

8. Say goodbye to canned beans from the store. Pressure can a variety of beans, lending your dishes a delightful texture and saving you from the hassle of soaking and boiling.

9. Organize your pressure-canned creations like a maestro arranges notes on a musical sheet. Keep similar items together for easy access, ensuring that each jar is showcased in your culinary repertoire.

10. Don't forget to label your jars with the same love you infuse into your creations. Include the date and contents, turning your pantry into a gallery of flavors waiting to be enjoyed.

Perfecting the Jam Consistency

Techniques for achieving the ideal jam texture

Creating the perfect jam is a skill that marries science and art. In this section, we'll unveil the secrets to achieving that ideal jam texture, ensuring your spreads are not just delicious but also boast a consistency that elevates your breakfast or tea time experience.

1. Selecting the Right Fruit: The foundation of exceptional jam lies in choosing ripe, high-quality fruit. Whether you're working with berries, stone fruits, or citrus, the key is to use fruit at its peak, ensuring a natural sweetness and vibrant flavor.

2. Balancing Pectin Levels: Pectin is the unsung hero of jam making, responsible for that delightful jelly-like consistency. Different fruits contain varying levels of pectin, and understanding this is crucial. For low-pectin fruits like strawberries, consider adding natural pectin boosters like apple cores or citrus peels.

3. The Sugar Content: Eh, the sweet sensation of sugar! Balancing sweetness is key to achieving the ideal jam texture. Too much sugar, and your jam may be overly sweet; too little, and it might not set properly. Experiment with sugar levels, considering the natural sweetness of your chosen fruit.

4. Mastering the Cook: Achieving the perfect jam texture is a delicate measure of temperature and time. Start with a rapid boil to activate the pectin, then simmer to allow the flavors to concentrate. Stir often to prevent sticking, and use a thermometer to ensure you hit that magical gel point.

5. Testing for Set: The wrinkle test, the spoon test – choose your jam-setting method! These simple tests help you determine if your jam has reached the desired texture. Remember, patience is key; rushing this stage might result in a runny disappointment.

6. Embrace Texture Variations. The beauty of homemade jam lies in its uniqueness. Don't be afraid to embrace variations in texture. Some may prefer a smoother finish, while others delight in chunky fruit bits. It's your jam, so tailor it to your taste

7. Cooling and Storing: Once your jam has achieved the perfect texture, allow it to cool slightly before transferring it to sterilized jars. Proper sealing and storage ensure your hard work is rewarded with months of flavorful bliss.

8. Troubleshooting Tips: Not every jam-making journey is without its bumps. If your jam turns out too runny, reheat and cook a bit longer. If it's too firm, consider adding a touch of liquid. Each batch is a learning experience, and the joy is in the process.

Low-sugar and no-sugar jam-making alternatives

Are you ready to revolutionize your jam-making game? Whether you're looking to cut down on sugar for health reasons or just exploring a different flavor profile, creating low-sugar and no-sugar jams is a rewarding journey. Let's dig into the alternatives and techniques that make this a sweet adventure.

1. The Magic of Pectin: Pectin, the unsung hero of jam-making, plays a crucial role in achieving that perfect gel without the need for excessive sugar. Opt for low-methoxyl pectin or natural sources like apples and citrus peels to boost the setting power.

2. Natural Sweeteners: Replace traditional white sugar with natural sweeteners like honey, maple syrup, or agave nectar. These alternatives not only add sweetness but also bring unique flavor undertones to your jams. Remember to adjust quantities based on sweetness preferences.

3. Fruit Selection Matters: Choose high-pectin fruits like apples, cranberries, or citrus fruits to naturally enhance the jam's texture and reduce the need for added sugars. Mixing low-pectin fruits with high-pectin ones can strike the perfect balance.

4. Experiment with Sugar Substitutes: Explore sugar substitutes like stevia, erythritol, or monk fruit to cut down on sugar content. Keep in mind that these substitutes have different sweetness levels, so start with small amounts and adjust to taste.

5. The Slow Cook Method: For a no-sugar-added approach, consider the slow cook method. This involves simmering the fruit until it naturally caramelizes, intensifying its sweetness. It requires patience but results in a jam that lets the fruit's natural sugars shine.

6. Chia Seeds and Gelatin: Chia seeds and gelatin are fantastic alternatives for achieving a gel-like consistency without excessive sugar. They not only aid in setting but also add nutritional value to your jams.

7. Balancing Act: Finding the right balance of sweetness without compromising texture can be a bit of a test. Taste as you go, and remember that the beauty of low-sugar and no-sugar jams lies in embracing the authentic flavors of the fruit.

8. Storage Considerations: Lower sugar content can impact the jam's shelf life. Store your creations in the refrigerator or consider small batches for more manageable consumption.

9. Labeling and Transparency: If you're sharing your jams or gifting them, be transparent about the sugar content. Labeling accurately ensures that recipients can enjoy your creations with awareness.

Turning preserves into gourmet delights

Are you ready to transform your preserves into culinary works of art? Let's unleash the gourmet potential hidden within your jars and discover how to impress your taste buds and those of your lucky guests.

1. Flavor Fusion: Elevate your preserves by experimenting with unexpected flavor combinations. Think beyond traditional pairings and consider adding herbs, spices, or even a splash of balsamic vinegar to create a blend of taste in each spoonful.

2. Infusing Elegance: Infuse your preserves with a touch of elegance by incorporating exotic ingredients. Vanilla beans, lavender, or even a hint of rosewater can add a luxurious layer to your creations, making them stand out on any gourmet spread.

3. Liqueur Love: Kick up the sophistication by introducing a splash of your favorite liqueur. Whether it's a berry preserve with a hint of Grand Marnier or a citrus marmalade infused with Limoncello, the addition of spirits can add depth and complexity.

4. Nuts for Texture: For a gourmet touch, consider adding finely chopped nuts. Almonds, pecans, or pistachios bring a delightful crunch to your preserves, creating a sensory experience that goes beyond the ordinary.

5. Cheese Pairing Pleasures: Elevate your preserves to gourmet status by exploring the world of cheese pairings. From a classic fig jam with brie to a spicy pepper jelly with cream cheese, the possibilities are endless and utterly delectable.

6. Savory Preserves: Break away from the sweet norm and venture into savory preserves. Try a tomato and chili jam, onion confit, or garlic and thyme-infused spread. These gourmet delights are perfect for enhancing everything from grilled meats to charcuterie boards.

7. Culinary Versatility: Gourmet preserves aren't just for spreading on toast. Use them as glazes for roasted meats, swirl them into yogurt, or incorporate them into salad dressings. Let your creativity flow, and watch as your preserves become culinary chameleons.

8. Presentation Matters: Elevate the overall gourmet experience by paying attention to presentation. Consider investing in elegant jars, add custom labels, and arrange your preserves thoughtfully to create a feast for the eyes.

9. Seasonal Inspirations: Let the seasons guide your gourmet creations. Experiment with flavors inspired by each season's bounty, ensuring your preserves are always in harmony with the freshest ingredients available.

10. Gourmet Gifting: Share the joy of gourmet preserves by turning them into thoughtful gifts. Personalize each jar, pair them with complementary treats, and watch as your creations become the highlight of any occasion.

Beyond Fruit Jams: Unconventional Spreads

Encouraging experimentation with savory spreads

1. Beyond Sweet Jams: While sweet jams have their charm, the savory world brings a whole new dimension to your canning journey. Think outside the sugar jar and welcome ingredients that resonates with the savory side of life.

2. The Flavor Palette: Just like an artist needs a palette, your savory spread adventure starts with key flavors. Garlic, herbs, spices, and umami-packed ingredients are your building blocks. Mix and match to create a blend of tastes.

3. Vegetable Bounty: Vegetables aren't just for the dinner plate; they're stars in your savory spreads. From sun-dried tomatoes to caramelized onions, let the vegetable bounty shine and add depth to your creations.

4. Bold and Brave: Savory spreads thrive on boldness. Don't be afraid to intensify flavors. Roasted garlic, smoked paprika, and chili peppers can transform your spreads into a bold and unforgettable experience.

5. Fusion Magic: Bring a world of flavors into your kitchen by experimenting with fusion spreads. Blend ingredients from different cuisines to create unique combinations that transport your taste buds to new horizons.

6. Versatility Rules: Savory spreads aren't just for your morning toast. Create versatile spreads that elevate snacks, appetizers, and main dishes. Let your jars be the secret ingredient that turns ordinary meals into extraordinary experiences.

7. Texture Play: Texture is a key player in the world of savory spreads. Experiment with chunky salsa-style spreads, creamy pâtés, and everything in between. The texture is your canvas; paint it with layers of deliciousness.

8. Preservation Magic: Savory spreads have a unique way of preserving the essence of the ingredients. Experience the magic of long-lasting flavors that intensify over time. Your jars are time capsules of culinary excellence.

9. Pairing Prowess: Discover the art of pairing savory spreads. Whether it's with artisanal cheeses, crusty bread, or grilled meats, let your spreads be the perfect companion that enhances the overall dining experience.

10. Seasonal Blending: Just like the seasons change, so can your savory spreads. Embrace what's fresh and in-season. Spring-inspired pea and mint spreads or fall's roasted pumpkin creations—let the seasons guide your creativity.

11. Recipe Remix: Recipes are a starting point, not a rulebook. Feel free to remix and tweak to match your taste buds. Your kitchen, your rules, and your savory spreads should reflect your unique culinary fingerprint.

12. Share the Joy: Experimentation is not meant to be kept a secret. Share your savory creations with friends, family, and fellow canners. Let your jars of joy find their way into the homes and hearts of those around you.

Recipes that go beyond traditional fruit-based jams

Canning has long been synonymous with fruit-based jams, but it's time to break free from tradition and let our creativity soar. Join us as we explore recipes that redefine the boundaries of what a spread can be, introducing exciting flavors and textures that go beyond the familiar realm of fruits.

Traditionally, jams have been sweet, but why limit ourselves to the sweet side of life? Get ready to savor the savory with recipes that introduce a whole new dimension to your canning adventures. From tangy chutneys to robust vegetable medleys, we're about to redefine what it means to spread something delightful on your morning toast.

Vegetables, often overlooked in the world of jams, take center stage in our unconventional spread recipes. Imagine a zesty tomato and basil concoction or a smoky roasted red pepper spread that adds a punch of flavor to your dishes.

Who said spreads are just for fruits and vegetables? Brace yourself for a delightful surprise as we explore recipes that incorporate protein-packed goodness. Picture a jar of bacon and caramelized onion jam or a savory chicken liver pâté spread that will make your taste buds dance. We're about to prove that spreads can be meaty and marvelous.

Let's take a journey around the world without leaving the comfort of your kitchen. Our recipes will draw inspiration from global flavors, infusing your spreads with the richness of ethnic cuisines. Think of a spicy mango-lime salsa or a Mediterranean-inspired olive tapenade – your taste buds are about to embark on a culinary adventure.

There's something special about a homemade gift from the heart. We'll wrap up this chapter by discussing how your unconventional spreads can become tokens of love. Imagine gifting a jar of spicy peach salsa or a garlic-herb goat cheese spread – these unique creations will surely bring joy to your friends and family.

Chapter 9

Troubleshooting and FAQs

Addressing Common Concerns

Troubleshooting guide for canning challenges

1. Jammed Jams and Jellies:

Challenge: You've noticed your jams are turning out thicker than expected.

Solution: This is a common issue, often caused by overcooking the fruit or using too much pectin. Adjust your cooking times, and consider using a bit less pectin in your next batch for the perfect spreadable consistency.

2. Cloudy Pickles:

Challenge: Your pickles are looking a bit cloudy, and you're aiming for that crisp clarity.

Solution: Cloudiness is typically the result of minerals in your water. Switch to distilled water or water that has been filtered to reduce mineral content. Additionally, ensure you're using the correct ratio of vinegar to water in your pickling brine.

3. Mysterious Mold:

Challenge: Uh-oh, there's an unwelcome guest in your canned goods - mold!

Solution: Proper hygiene is your ally here. Make sure jars are thoroughly cleaned and sterilized before use. Also, check that the headspace and processing times are accurate for the recipe you're following. Adjustments here can help keep mold at bay.

4. Siphoning Woes:

Challenge: You've noticed liquid escaping from your jars during processing.

Solution: Siphoning occurs when there's too much liquid in the jar, and it spills out during processing. Leave the recommended headspace, and be cautious not to overtighten the lids, as this can also lead to siphoning. Tighten the lids "fingertip tight" for optimal results.

5. Color Conundrums:

Challenge: The vibrant colors of your fruits and vegetables are fading post-canning.

Solution: The culprit here is often excessive heat during processing. Lower the processing temperature and duration to preserve the beautiful hues of your produce.

6. Lost Crunch in Pickles:

Challenge: Your pickles have lost their satisfying crunch.

Solution: Fear not, crunch-seekers! Ensure you're using the freshest cucumbers, and add grape leaves or pickle crisp granules to your jars. These additives help maintain that sought-after crispiness.

7. Uneven Heating:

Challenge: Some jars in your batch are hotter than others during processing.

Solution: Uneven heating can occur due to inadequate water circulation in your canner. Arrange jars with enough space between them for water to flow freely. And remember, patience is key during the heating process.

8. Floating Fruit Blues:

Challenge: The fruit in your jams and preserves is floating towards the top.

Solution: This happens when the fruit is less dense than the syrup or liquid. To combat this, let your fruit sit in the syrup for a few minutes before processing to release air bubbles and ensure you're filling jars with the recommended headspace.

9. Seal Struggles:

Challenge: Not all your jars sealed properly.

Solution: First, check for any nicks or cracks on the jar rims that might impede proper sealing. Ensure the lids are in good condition, and apply the right amount of pressure when securing them. Always follow the recommended processing times for a secure seal.

10. Off-Taste Surprises:

Challenge: Your canned goods have an unexpected off-taste.

Solution: This can happen if your jars weren't cleaned thoroughly before filling. Always wash jars with hot, soapy water and rinse well before using. Additionally, avoid using rusty or damaged canning equipment, as this can impact the taste of your final product.

FAQs for quick problem-solving

1. Q: Why is my jam too runny?

A: Runny jams can be the result of undercooking or not using enough pectin. Ensure you follow the recommended cooking times and use the correct amount of pectin according to your recipe. If the issue persists, consider adding a bit more pectin in your next batch.

2. Q: How do I prevent my pickles from turning soft?

A: Soft pickles may be caused by overripe cucumbers or insufficient brine strength. Choose firm, fresh cucumbers, and double-check your brine ratio. Adding a grape leaf or pickle crisp granules to each jar can also help maintain that desired crunch.

3. Q: What causes mold in canned goods?

A: Mold can creep in if jars aren't adequately cleaned and sterilized or if there's not enough headspace. Make sure to thoroughly clean and sterilize your jars, leaving the recommended headspace for proper air circulation.

4. Q: Can I reprocess jars that didn't seal?

A: Unfortunately, no. Once the canning process is complete, attempting to reseal jars is not recommended. Instead, refrigerate any unsealed jars and consume their contents promptly.

5. Q: How do I prevent siphoning during processing?

A: Siphoning occurs when there's too much liquid in the jar. Ensure you leave the correct headspace and avoid overtightening the lids. Tighten them "fingertip tight" for optimal results.

6. Q: Why are my fruits floating to the top of the jars?

A: Fruits can float if they're less dense than the syrup or liquid. Let your fruit sit in the syrup for a few minutes before processing to release air bubbles, and always follow the recommended headspace.

7. Q: How can I fix jars that didn't seal properly?

A: Check for nicks or cracks on the jar rims and ensure the lids are in good condition. Apply the right amount of pressure when securing the lids, and always follow the recommended processing times for a secure seal.

8. Q: Why do my canned goods have an off-taste?

A: An off-taste might be due to inadequate cleaning of jars before filling or using rusty or damaged canning equipment. Thoroughly wash jars and avoid using compromised equipment.

9. Q: What's the ideal storage for canned goods?

A: Store your canned goodies in a cool, dark, and dry place. Avoid direct sunlight, as it can alter flavors and affect the quality of your preserves.

10. Q: Can I use glass jars with chips or cracks?

A: Never use jars with chips or cracks. These imperfections can lead to seal failures and pose safety risks during processing.

Building confidence in every canner

Embarking on your canning adventure can feel like stepping into uncharted territory. Fear not, for every great canner had a beginning. Embrace the learning curve with open arms, knowing that every jar of goodness is a step toward mastering the art.

Confidence begins with knowing your ingredients intimately. Familiarize yourself with the nuances of each fruit, vegetable, or spice you choose. Let your taste buds be your guide, and soon you'll be orchestrating a blend of flavors that dance on the palates of those lucky enough to savor your creations. A confident canner is a well-equipped canner. Take the time to master each tool, from ladles to lids. Know the ins and outs of your canning kit, for in that familiarity lies the key to a seamless canning process.

An organized workspace is the cornerstone of confidence. Set the stage for success by arranging your ingredients and tools with intention. A clutter-free zone not only makes the canning process smoother but also elevates your confidence to new heights.

Sterilization may sound daunting, but it's your ally in the quest for safety and confidence. Embrace the Zen of cleanliness, and your jars will become sanctuaries for the delicious concoctions within. A clean jar is a canvas waiting for the brushstrokes of your culinary creativity.

Recipes are your trusted companions, not strict dictators. Understand the language they speak and feel free to experiment within the boundaries they provide. As you decode the culinary lexicon, you'll find the freedom to add your signature touch to every jar.

Every canner encounter challenge; it's part of the journey. Instead of viewing them as setbacks, see them as opportunities to hone your skills. Troubleshooting with panache transforms obstacles into stepping stones toward canning mastery.

As you open that first jar of your meticulously crafted preserves, savor the sweet taste of success. Your journey from novice to confident canner is a testament to your dedication and passion. Confidence is not merely a destination; it's a companion on your ongoing canning odyssey.

Reducing Food Waste Through Canning

Highlighting the role of home canning in reducing food waste

The journey of our food from the farm to our forks is an interesting process, but it's marred by the disheartening reality of waste. Fruits and vegetables deemed "imperfect" by commercial standards find themselves discarded, and kitchens often witness the tragic demise of forgotten produce. It's time to flip the script and let canning be our instrument of change.

Home canning is a beacon of hope in the fight against food waste. Those extra tomatoes from the garden, the bounty of berries begging to be plucked, and the surplus of seasonal vegetables—all find purpose within the walls of our jars. Waste not, want not—a can opener's creed that transforms excess into excellence.

Enter the world of preservation, where perishable ingredients waltz into jars, emerging as timeless delicacies. Witness the magical transformation as strawberries burst forth in jams, and pickles become the spirited dancers in our culinary ball.

Canning transforms the way we view ingredients. It compels us to become mindful consumers, appreciating the seasonal bounty and fostering a connection with our food. No longer are fruits and vegetables fleeting; they become captured moments in time, awaiting their release in a burst of flavor. Ever found a lonely carrot or a neglected apple at the bottom of your refrigerator? Fear not, for a canner sees potential where others see waste.

Every overlooked ingredient is a can of second chances, ready to reclaim its place in the spotlight of your pantry. Picture a pantry that transcends seasons—a treasure trove of jars bursting with summer's sunshine and autumn's warmth. Home canning bestows upon us the gift of abundance beyond the limitations of the harvest season.

As a canner, your impact extends beyond the confines of your kitchen. Share your jars, share your love, and witness the ripples of change within your community. Each jar is a testimonial to the power of one individual to make a difference in the global fight against food waste.

Encouraging canners to embrace sustainability in their canning practices

Imagine your backyard or a local farmers' market bursting with the vibrant hues of ripe produce. As canners, we are the conductors orchestrating a legacy of sustainability. By choosing local, seasonal ingredients, we minimize the carbon footprint, reduce transportation emissions, and celebrate the rhythm of nature.

Sustainability extends beyond the ingredients and spills into the realm of packaging. Opt for reusable glass jars, breathing life into the concept of *"reduce, reuse, recycle."* As we seal the essence of summer into our jars, we're also making a pact to reduce plastic waste and tread lightly on our planet. In the world of canning, nothing goes to waste. Scraps, peels, and cores become secret ingredients in the alchemy of flavors. We encourage you, dear canner, to embrace the thrifty jar wizard within. Compost what can't be canned, turning waste into nutrient-rich gold for your garden.

The water bath canner is our trusted ally, but let's use it judiciously. By adopting water conservation practices during canning, we not only reduce our environmental impact but also pay homage to the life-giving essence of water. Capture rainwater, reuse canning water for plants – let every drop count.

Sustainable canning is more than just a practice; it's a mindset. Embrace root-to-stem wisdom, where every part of the ingredient has a purpose. Turn carrot tops into pesto, pickle watermelon rinds, and discover the extraordinary potential of the oft-overlooked leaves, peels, and stems.

Imagine a community compost where canners gather, sharing not just recipes but also compostable waste. By collectively composting, we create nutrient-rich soil, closing the loop of sustainability. The bond between the earth and our jars strengthens, fostering a sense of community responsibility. Sustainability transcends our kitchens and extends to the fields. Support local farmers committed to sustainable practices. By doing so, we champion biodiversity, reduce the need for harmful pesticides, and contribute to the resilience of local ecosystems.

Our role as canners is not only to preserve the present but also to inspire the next generation. Teach the art of sustainable canning to children and grandchildren, sowing the seeds of eco-consciousness. With each passing jar, we pass down a legacy of respect for nature.

Eco-Friendly Canning: Tips and Tricks

Exploring environmentally friendly packaging options

1.The Jar: Behold, the humble glass jar – a timeless companion in our canning adventures. This stalwart vessel not only withstands the tests of time but also emerges as an eco-warrior. Reusable and endlessly recyclable, it champions the cause of sustainability with a resounding clink. Let's raise our jars to this unsung hero of the pantry.

2. Lid Choices: Our lids play a crucial role in the canning ballet. Opt for lids made from materials like BPA-free tin-plated steel, which can be recycled. Better yet, explore reusable options like Tattler lids. These champions can be used time and again, sparing the landfill from unnecessary waste. The lid, after all, is the guardian of flavors and the protector of our Earth.

3. Waxing Poetic: Consider the time-honored practice of sealing jars with wax. Beeswax or soy wax offers an eco-friendly alternative to disposable lids. This rustic touch not only adds a poetic charm to your canning but also contributes to the reduction of single-use plastics in your pantry.

4. Fabric Covers: Let's add a dash of color to our pantry, shall we? Fabric covers, secured with twine or rubber bands, not only bring a touch of rustic elegance to your preserves but also eliminate the need for disposable covers. Choose vibrant, reusable fabrics to wrap your jars – a feast for both the eyes and the Earth.

5. The Art of Tying: Ah, the simple pleasure of tying twine around our jars! Nature's twine, made from materials like jute or hemp, serves as a biodegradable and aesthetically pleasing alternative to plastic. As we secure our jars with these eco-friendly ties, we nod to simplicity and sustainability.

6. Labels: Organization is the heartbeat of efficient canning. When it comes to labeling, consider reusable options like chalkboard labels or tags tied with twine. Bid farewell to single-use stickers and usher in a new era of sustainability where labels can be erased and rewritten, aligning perfectly with the ever-changing seasons of your pantry.

7. Upcycled Elegance: Why bid adieu to jars once their original purpose is fulfilled? Embrace the art of upcycling. Turn your jars into elegant storage containers, vases, or candleholders. By doing so, we not only reduce waste but also infuse our homes with the charm of repurposed creativity.

8. Unwrapping the Packaging Puzzle: In the age of online shopping, the packaging becomes a critical piece of the puzzle. Opt for companies that use eco-friendly packaging materials, minimizing plastic and prioritizing recyclable materials. By making mindful choices, we can be eco-conscious even in the virtual aisles.

9. The Local Touch: Support local artisans and companies that prioritize sustainability in their packaging. Seek out jams, pickles, and preserves packaged in environmentally friendly materials. By doing so, you champion not only your local economy but also sustainable practices in the broader food industry.

10. DIY Craftiness: For the crafty canners among us, consider crafting your packaging. From fabric wraps to personalized tags, infuse your unique touch into every jar. By investing time and creativity, you not only reduce reliance on disposable materials but also turn canning into a truly personalized art.

Reducing energy consumption during canning process

1.Efficient Equipment Choices: In our arsenal of canning tools, selecting energy-efficient equipment is the first step towards sustainable preservation. Consider investing in canners that matches your batch size, minimizing excess energy consumption. Opt for induction cooktops, which channel heat directly to the pot, ensuring no energy goes to waste.

2. Gas vs. Electric: As the flames dance beneath our canning pots, we must ponder the eternal question: gas or electric? Gas stovetops offer precise control and instant heat, whereas electric stovetops tend to have a slower response time. Choose the worthy partner that suits your rhythm while being mindful of energy efficiency.

3. Timing is Everything: Efficiency in batch processing is an art that canners must master. Plan your canning sessions to maximize each batch, minimizing the time your energy source is in use. This strategic move ensures the preservation of flavors without squandering unnecessary energy.

4. Adjusting Heat Intensity: Achieving the perfect simmer is akin to orchestrating a sweet expertise in your kitchen. Adjust the heat intensity precisely to maintain the simmer without unnecessary boiling. Not only does this save energy, but it also safeguards the delicate textures and flavors of your precious preserves.

5. Lid Lifting: Ever witnessed a canner's ballet of lifting lids? Embrace this choreography while minimizing heat loss. Lift lids strategically and avoid excessive peeking to maintain a consistent temperature. By doing so, you not only conserve energy but also ensure the safety and quality of your canned treasures.

6. Preserving Heat: The magic of canning lies in the jars' warm embrace. Utilize residual heat to your advantage. Turn off the heat source a few minutes before your preserves are done and let the jars bask in the warmth. This small act can significantly reduce energy usage while preserving flavors to perfection.

7. Water Wisdom: For water bath canners, wisdom lies in conserving water. Rather than letting the tap run endlessly to fill your canning pot, collect water in a large container and use only what you need. This simple practice ensures water efficiency without compromising the safety of your canning process.

8. Joining Forces: Consider hosting canning parties with friends and neighbors. A shared canning endeavor not only fosters community spirit but also allows you to split the energy costs. It's a win-win situation where the joy of canning is multiplied, and the environmental impact is minimized.

9. Future-Forward Investment: For those with a passion for the future, investing in solar or alternative energy sources can be a game-changer. Imagine harnessing the power of the sun to fuel your canning adventures! While a substantial investment, the long-term benefits for both your wallet and the environment are undeniable.

Long-term ecological impact of sustainable canning practices

Adopting sustainable farming practices for your canning ingredients lays the foundation for an ecologically conscious canning experience. In your canning garden, let biodiversity reign supreme. A diverse array of plants not only enhances the flavors of your preserves but also nurtures a healthier ecosystem. It's a subtle yet impactful way to contribute to the overall health of our planet.

Consider the ecological footprint of your packaging choices. Opt for materials that are kind to the environment, such as reusable glass jars and eco-friendly lids. These choices not only preserve the integrity of your creations but also extend your commitment to sustainability beyond the kitchen. Align your canning sessions with the natural rhythm of the seasons. By doing so, you reduce the need for energy-intensive climate control in your kitchen. Let nature guide your canning calendar, creating a beautiful atmosphere that mirrors the Earth's cycles.

Integrate the three R's into your canning routine. Reduce waste by utilizing surplus produce for canning, reuse jars and lids whenever possible, and recycle responsibly. These simple yet impactful practices echo the larger environmental ethos and showcase your commitment to a greener future. Your flow with the flames can be an elegant ballet that minimizes your carbon footprint. Choose energy-efficient appliances, monitor your energy usage, and consider alternative energy sources where possible. A mindful approach to energy consumption contributes to a healthier planet.

Consider forming or joining canning communities. Shared resources, knowledge, and experiences not only strengthen the bonds of a community but also pave the way for collective ecological consciousness. A united front of canners can bring about positive change at a broader scale. Wield your canning wand to perform food waste minimization. Transform kitchen scraps into compost, enriching the soil and completing the cycle of sustainability. As a canner, you hold the power to reduce food waste and nourish the Earth in one fell swoop.

As a passionate canner, your knowledge is a precious legacy. Share your sustainable canning practices with future generations. By passing down the wisdom of eco-friendly preservation, you contribute to a world where respect for the environment is a cornerstone of everyday life.

As we conclude this exploration of sustainable canning practices, envision the ripple effect of your choices. Each jar you seal with care and each ingredient you grow sustainably send out waves of gratitude to the Earth. Your canning kitchen is not just a space for culinary creativity; it's a harbor where passion and sustainability coexist.

Culinary Artistry: Presenting Canned Goods

Creative ideas for visually appealing canned goods

1.The Art of Layering: Elevate your canned goods by embracing the art of layering. Consider the color palette of your ingredients and arrange them in visually appealing layers within the jar. From vibrant jams to pickled medleys, layering adds depth and allure.

2. Rainbow Jams: Take your fruit jams to the next level by embracing the full spectrum of colors. Create rainbow jams using an assortment of fruits, carefully layering them to showcase the beauty of each hue. A jar filled with the vividness of nature is a treat for both the eyes and the taste buds.

3. Pickled Precision: Pickling isn't just a preservation method; it's an art form. Experiment with pickling different vegetables to create visually striking patterns. From alternating colors to carefully sliced designs, transform your pickled goods into geometric wonders that dazzle on the shelf.

4. Herb-Infused Elegance: Bring a touch of nature into your jars by infusing your creations with herbs. Whether it's a sprig of rosemary in savory spreads or basil leaves in fruit preserves, the addition of greenery not only enhances the flavor but also adds a touch of visual elegance.

5. Floral Finesse: Edible flowers aren't just for gardens; they can be stars in your canned goods too. Experiment with blooms like violets, pansies, or nasturtiums to create visually stunning pickled flowers or floral-infused jams. It's a celebration of nature's beauty in every jar.

6. Citrus Zest Extravaganza: Citrus zest isn't just a flavor booster; it's a visual delight. Infuse your canned goods with citrus zests, adding both brightness and texture. The vibrant specks of zest create a lively, dynamic appearance that transforms your creations into works of art.

7. Jam Artistry: Take your jam-making to the level of artistry by turning each jar into a gem. Use contrasting fruits to create swirls and patterns, resembling strokes of a brush. Your jams become edible paintings that tell a story of flavor and aesthetics.

8. Seasonal Themes: Embrace the changing seasons as opportunities to theme your canned goods. Create preserves that mirror the colors and flavors of each season. Whether it's the

warmth of autumn spices or the freshness of spring fruits, let your canning reflect the beauty around you.

9. Monochrome Magic: Sometimes, less is more. Explore the world of monochrome magic by selecting ingredients within a similar color family. This minimalist approach creates a sophisticated, elegant appearance that is both visually pleasing and showcases the simplicity of your ingredients.

10. Customized Labels: Complete the visual allure of your canned creations with customized labels. Personalize each jar with charming labels that reflect the care and creativity you've poured into your canning process. A beautifully labeled jar is a gift both to yourself and those you share it with.

11. The Joy of Gifting: Extend the joy of visually appealing canned goods by sharing them with friends and family. Create custom gift sets, combining flavors and aesthetics. Your creations become not just preserves but expressions of your creativity and love.

Tips on labeling and personalizing canned items

1.Labeling Essentials: A good label should include the name of your creation, the date it was canned, and, if relevant, any special notes or ingredients. This ensures clarity and helps you keep track of your pantry inventory.

2. The Beauty of Handwriting: In the digital age, there's a certain charm in the handwritten. Consider adding a touch of nostalgia by personally writing your labels. Whether you have elegant cursive or bold block letters, your handwriting adds an authentic and sentimental dimension to your canned goods.

3. Creative Naming: Naming your creations is an art in itself. Infuse personality and creativity into your labels by coming up with unique and catchy names for your canned goods. Playful names not only make your jars memorable but also reflect the spirit of your culinary endeavor.

4. Colorful Contrasts: The visual appeal of your labels matters just as much as the contents inside. Opt for contrasting colors between the label and the jar to make your creations visually striking. Dark labels on light jars or vice versa create a vibrant contrast that catches the eye.

5. Custom Illustrations: Transform your labels into mini masterpieces by incorporating custom illustrations. Whether it's a doodle of the main ingredients or a representation of the flavor profile, adding artwork to your labels elevates the visual experience and showcases your creativity.

6. Personal Messages: Consider adding a personal touch by including brief messages on your labels. It could be a heartfelt thank-you note, a quirky description, or even serving suggestions. These personal messages create a connection between you and the eventual consumer of your canned delights.

7. Seasonal Themes: Just as you theme your canned goods, why not extend the theme to your labels? Create labels that harmonize with the seasons. Think warm tones for autumn, pastels for spring, and cool blues for summer. Seasonal labels make your pantry a dynamic reflection of the passing months.

8. Elegant Fonts: The font you choose contributes significantly to the overall aesthetic. Experiment with different fonts to find one that complements the style of your canned products. From classic serif fonts to playful scripts, the right typography enhances the visual appeal of your labels.

9. Sustainable Labeling: Extend your commitment to sustainability to your labeling choices. Opt for eco-friendly materials for your labels, such as recycled paper or even reusable tags. A sustainable approach ensures that your passion for canning aligns with your values for a greener planet.

10. Labeling Kits: Transform labeling into a family or friend activity by creating labeling kits. Gather your loved ones, provide materials like markers, stickers, and labels, and let everyone contribute to the labeling process. It's a fun way to involve others in your canning passion.

11. Sharing the Joy: As you label your creations, consider the joy of sharing them with others. Gift your canned goods with pride, knowing that the personalized labels not only showcase your craftsmanship but also make your gifts extra special.

Viewing home-canned goods as artisanal creations

1. From Pantry: It's time to redefine the perception of home-canned goods. No longer confined to the pantry as convenient staples, envision your jars as artisanal expressions of your culinary prowess. Each jar tells a unique story, crafted with care and creativity that rivals any gourmet creation.

2. The Craftsmanship of Canning: Consider your canning process as a culinary masterwork, where you, the canner, are the conductor orchestrating a harmonious blend of flavors. From the selection of produce to the infusion of spices, every step is a note in the melody of your artisanal creation.

3. Quality Ingredients: Just as a painter carefully selects their palette, a canner chooses quality ingredients. Your fruits, vegetables, and spices are the vibrant colors that breathe life into your culinary creations. Seek out the freshest produce and premium spices to elevate your creations.

4. Balancing Flavors: Artisanal creations are known for their balance of flavors, and home-canned goods should be no exception. Experiment with the proportions of sweetness, acidity, and spice to create a blend of tastes that dance on the palate and leave a lasting impression.

5. Presentation Matters: Artisanal products are as much about presentation as they are about taste. Consider how you present your jars — from the choice of jar shapes to the meticulousness of your labeling. Aesthetics matter; let your jars be visually appealing, enticing others to explore the treasures within.

6. Limited Batches: Artisanal goods are often produced in limited quantities, adding an air of exclusivity. Embrace this concept in your canning journey. Instead of mass production, focus on limited batches of unique creations. This not only enhances the perceived value but also allows you to experiment freely.

7. Pairing and Serving Suggestions: Just as a sommelier suggests wine pairings, think about how your home-canned goods can complement various dishes. Include serving suggestions on your labels, inspiring those who enjoy your creations to elevate their culinary experiences by incorporating your jars into diverse recipes.

8. Your Signature Touch: Consider developing a signature style or flavor that sets your creations apart. Whether it's a special spice blend, a unique combination of fruits, or an unconventional pickling method, your signature touch adds a layer of identity to your artisanal jars.

9. Sharing the Art: Don't keep your culinary masterpieces hidden away. Share the art of home canning by gifting your artisanal creations to friends and family. Let your jars be not only a source of sustenance but also a culinary showcase that sparks conversations and appreciation.

10. Artisanal Canning Communities: Join or create communities that celebrate the art of home canning. Share your experiences, exchange ideas, and revel in the creativity of fellow canners. The collective passion of a community can inspire and elevate the art of canning for all involved.

11. Artisanal Canning Events: Consider organizing or participating in artisanal canning events. Whether it's a local farmers' market or a community fair, these gatherings provide a platform for you to showcase your creations, garner feedback, and inspire others to view home canning through an artisanal lens.

Canning as a Thoughtful Gift

The sentimentality of gifting home-canned goods

When you gift a jar of home-canned goods, you're not just presenting someone with food; you're gifting them a piece of your heart. There's an inherent love that permeates every layer of the canning process, and that sentiment is passed along to the lucky recipient. Unlike store-bought items, homemade gifts have a personal touch that money can't buy. As a canner, you're not just preserving fruits or pickles; you're encapsulating memories, effort, and the unique essence of your kitchen in every jar.

Not all jars are created equal, and not all recipients have the same taste buds. Tailor your home-canned gifts to the preferences of the person receiving them. Whether it's a friend who loves spicy pickles or a relative with a sweet tooth, let your jars be a reflection of the recipient's tastes.

Consider the occasions when gifting your creations. Whether it's a birthday, holiday, or a simple gesture of appreciation, your jars can elevate the celebration. Homemade gifts have a magical way of making ordinary moments extraordinary. The packaging is as crucial as the contents when it comes to gifting home-canned goods. Consider using decorative labels, colorful ribbons, or personalized tags. A beautifully presented jar not only entices but also communicates the thought and care behind the gift.

Home canning allows you to carry on family traditions with each jar. Consider gifting jars of recipes passed down through generations. It's a beautiful way to preserve not just the recipe but also the spirit of family and tradition. Go beyond a single jar and curate a homemade gift basket. Include a variety of your canned goods, perhaps paired with artisanal cheeses, crusty bread, or other complementary treats. The result? A culinary gift basket that's as delightful as it is heartfelt.

Take the time to create personalized labels and heartfelt messages for your jars. Whether it's a witty tagline, a warm message, or even a simple "Made with Love," these personal touches make your gifts all the more special. Consider gifting jars unexpectedly. A surprise jar left on a friend's doorstep, a small token of appreciation for a neighbor, or a spontaneous gift for a colleague can spread joy in unexpected ways. Your jars become delightful surprises that brighten someone's day.

Witnessing the joy your homemade gifts bring is a reward in itself. As a canner, you're not just preserving food; you're preserving happiness. The act of giving becomes a reciprocal joy, enriching both the giver and the receiver.

Create gifting traditions around your home-canned goods. Whether it's an annual holiday jar exchange or a summer pickling party, these traditions become a part of your canning legacy, shared with friends and family alike.

In conclusion, gifting home-canned goods transcends the act of giving food; it's about sharing love, memories, and the essence of your kitchen. Your jars become vessels of sentimentality, nourishing not only the body but also the soul of those fortunate enough to receive them.

Ideas for creating themed canning gift baskets

The paramount step in crafting a sensational canning gift basket is to choose a theme. Consider the tastes and preferences of the recipient. Whether it's a celebration of summer flavors, a cozy winter collection, or an exotic international theme, your chosen theme sets the stage for a culinary adventure.

For the sweet tooth in your life, consider crafting a jam-packed gift basket. Include an assortment of your finest fruit jams, marmalades, and preserves. Think beyond the usual suspects; experiment with unique flavor combinations like peach and lavender or raspberry and balsamic. Your recipient will have a richness of sweetness to enjoy.

For those who savor the tangy and savory, a pickle-themed basket is a pick that won't disappoint. Fill your basket with an array of pickled delights—cucumbers, beets, jalapeños, and perhaps a jar of your secret spicy pickled green beans. This basket promises a journey through the tangy side of your canning repertoire.

Craft a basket that warms both the heart and the belly. Fill it with jars of hearty soups, stews, and chilis. Imagine the delight of your recipient as they cozy up to a homemade bowl of your signature chicken noodle soup or a robust vegetarian chili. It's a winter feast in a basket, ready to thaw even the chilliest of evenings.

Take your recipient on a culinary journey with an exotic-themed gift basket. Infuse your jars with flavors from around the world—perhaps a jar of zesty Moroccan preserved lemons, fiery Indian chutneys, or a taste of the Mediterranean with sun-dried tomatoes and olives. Each jar becomes a passport to a new and exciting taste adventure.

Start the day right with a breakfast-themed gift basket. Include jars of your finest fruit preserves, honey-infused spreads, and maybe even a jar of homemade granola. Your recipient will appreciate the effort you've put into making their mornings extra special.

For the spice enthusiasts, a hot sauce-themed basket is a fiery delight. Experiment with different peppers and spices to create a range of heat levels. Include a variety of hot sauces, from mild to scorching, providing your recipient with the perfect condiment for any culinary escapade.

Elevate tea time with an elegant gift basket. Craft infused syrups using herbs from your garden and pair them with loose-leaf tea blends. Imagine the joy of your recipient as they sip on a cup of your lavender-infused honey syrup in their favorite tea.

Craft baskets that celebrate the changing seasons. In the spring, think floral-infused syrups and delicate jams. Summer baskets could burst with sun-kissed fruits and vibrant pickles. Fall baskets might feature spiced apple butter and hearty soups. Embrace the seasonal bounty to create truly special gifts.

Transform ordinary pizza nights into extraordinary culinary gem. Craft a basket with homemade pizza sauce, pickled toppings, and perhaps a jar of fiery chili oil. Your recipient will thank you for turning their pizza nights into a gourmet experience.

Ensure your gift basket is a feast for the eyes as well. Add personal touches like decorative labels, themed tags, or even a handwritten recipe for a dish that perfectly complements your canned goods. The presentation is the final flourish that elevates your basket to a true work of edible art.

Tips for packaging and presenting canned items as cherished gifts

The prominent step in turning your canned creations into cherished gifts is to pay attention to presentation. Consider the aesthetic appeal of your jars. Choose clean, uniform jars and ensure they are spotlessly clean before filling them. A visually appealing jar is the fabric upon which your culinary jewel is displayed.

Labels are not just about identifying the contents; they're an opportunity to infuse your personality into the gift. Create custom labels that reflect the theme or flavor of your creation. Handwritten notes or quirky taglines add a personal touch that says, "This was made with love, just for you." Upgrade your jars with the simple elegance of themed ribbons or rustic twine. Choose colors that complement the contents or match the occasion. For a holiday touch, consider red and green; for a rustic feel, opt for twine or burlap. The way you tie your jars can turn them into individual pieces of art.

Transform your canned goods into a cohesive gift by placing them in a charming basket. Select a basket that suits the theme—*wicker* for a rustic feel, a *wire basket* for a modern touch, or a *festive basket* for holiday gifts. Arrange your jars thoughtfully, creating a visually stunning display. Gift tags are the unsung heroes of gift-giving. Create DIY tags that match the theme or occasion. Incorporate small, heartfelt messages, or attach a recipe card suggesting delightful ways to use the canned contents. It's a small detail that adds immeasurable charm.

Consider the season when packaging your canned goods. For spring, adorn jars with pastel ribbons; for autumn, opt for warm, earthy tones. Let the colors of nature guide your packaging choices, creating gifts that harmonize with the beauty of the moment.

Enhance the usability of your gift by including practical accessories. Attach a wooden spoon for jams and preserves, a set of recipe cards, or even a stylish bottle opener for pickled items. These thoughtful additions elevate your gift from delightful to indispensable. Add visual interest by incorporating jars of various sizes and shapes. Mix and match to create a dynamic ensemble that captures attention. A diverse array of jars not only looks appealing but also showcases the range of your canning prowess.

Go beyond individual jars and create themed combinations. Pair a jar of homemade salsa with pickled jalapeños and include a bag of artisan tortilla chips for a Mexican-inspired fiesta. The synergy of flavors turns your gift into a culinary experience. Infuse your packaging with storytelling elements. Include a brief note or tag that shares the inspiration behind your creation or a fun anecdote from your canning journey. This personal touch not only adds depth to the gift but also invites the recipient into your world of canning passion.

Advise your recipients on proper storage to maintain the freshness of your canned items. Include tips on refrigeration, shelf life, and usage. This practical information ensures that your gift is not only delightful upon receipt but continues to bring joy in the days to come.

Consider eco-friendly packaging options. Utilize reusable jars, fabric wraps, or biodegradable materials. Not only does this align with sustainable practices, but it also adds a touch of conscientiousness to your thoughtful gifts.

Reflecting on Your Canning Journey

Reflecting on your unique canning experiences

1. The Heartfelt Journey: Consider the transformative journey each ingredient takes from your kitchen to the jar. Reflect on the joyous moments spent harvesting fresh produce, the anticipation as fruits simmer in bubbling pots, and the comforting aroma that fills your kitchen. Your canning adventure is a narrative, and each jar is a chapter in that story.

2. Lessons in Patience: As you reflect, acknowledge the lessons in patience that canning imparts. The gentle simmering, the aromatic infusion of spices, and the gradual melding of flavors teach us the value of waiting for perfection. The sealed jar is a reward for your patience, a reminder that good things come to those who wait.

3. Harmonizing Tastes and Memories: Think about the unique blend of flavors that flow within each jar. Your hands have orchestrated a melody of tastes, blending ingredients to create a harmonious composition. Reflect on the memories associated with each flavor—perhaps a family recipe passed down or a twist that makes it entirely your own.

4. Joy in Imperfection: Homemade goodness is characterized by its quirks, and each imperfection is a badge of authenticity. Reflect on the times when a jam didn't set as expected or when pickles turned out crunchier than planned. These quirks are the signatures of homemade delights, reminding us that perfection lies in the imperfect.

5. Shared Moments: Consider the moments of shared joy during your canning escapades. Whether it's the laughter with a friend while chopping vegetables or the quiet companionship of family members gathered around the stove, canning becomes a bonding experience. Reflect on the people who have shared these moments with you, creating a tapestry of shared memories.

6. Nostalgia in Every Jar: Reflect on the traditions and heritage woven into every jar. Is there a recipe handed down through generations, a technique learned from a wise elder, or a spice blend that echoes cultural roots? Your canning journey is a vessel that carries forward the richness of tradition, preserving flavors that connect you to the past.

7. A Personal Time Capsule: Each jar is a time capsule, capturing moments in your life. Reflect on the jars created for special occasions—a jar of preserves made to celebrate an anniversary, pickles prepared for a summer picnic, or jams crafted for the joy of welcoming a new season. These jars become markers of milestones, encapsulating the essence of that particular moment.

8. Canning Adventures: Recall the canning adventures that took you from conundrums to triumphs. Reflect on the times you faced unexpected challenges, whether it was tackling a surplus of produce or troubleshooting a stubborn set. Each hurdle turned into a triumph, adding layers to your canning expertise.

9. The Giftable Magic: Think about the magic that happens when jars become heartfelt presents. Reflect on the joy of gifting a jar to a friend, the delight in their eyes as they receive your creation, and the shared happiness that stems from homemade generosity. Your jars are not just culinary creations; they are tokens of love and thoughtfulness.

10. An Ever-Evolving Craft: Consider how your canning craft has evolved over time. Reflect on the new techniques you've embraced, the innovative recipes you've dared to try, and the growth that comes with each batch. Your canning journey is an ever-evolving exploration, and each jar is a testament to your commitment to the craft.

11. Future Adventures: As you reflect on your unique canning experiences, let your thoughts extend to the future. Anticipate the jars yet to come, the recipes waiting to be discovered, and the memories yet to be made. Your canning journey is a continuum, and the best may be just around the corner.

Highlighting the growth and resilience gained through home canning

1. The Seed of Curiosity: Consider the very first jar you embarked upon. It all began with a seed of curiosity—perhaps sparked by a family tradition, a love for fresh produce, or an innate desire to craft something special. Reflect on how this seed grew into a full-fledged passion for canning, nurturing your curiosity into a thriving interest.

2. Patience in Every Bubble: As your fruits bubbled and your pickles brined, you unknowingly embraced a lesson in patience. The slow simmer of perseverance taught you that good things come to those who patiently wait. Each jar became a metaphorical representation of the endurance gained through the canning process.

3. From Setbacks to Solutions: Think about the moments when a recipe didn't unfold as expected. Instead of frustration, consider how these setbacks became stepping stones for growth. Troubleshooting challenges in canning equipped you with a valuable skill set, transforming mishaps into opportunities to learn and adapt.

4. The Resilient Seal: Pressure canning, as the name suggests, introduces an element of pressure and uncertainty. Yet, as every successfully sealed jar attests, you conquered this challenge. Reflect on the resilience required to navigate uncertainties, and how each sealed jar is a proof to your ability to overcome pressure and emerge triumphant.

5. A Jar Full of Learning: Your canning journey is not merely a series of recipes; it's a continuous educational experience. Each jar holds the wisdom gained from exploring new techniques, trying innovative recipes, and understanding the science behind the preservation process. Reflect on how your journey has become a school of its own, with jars as textbooks filled with knowledge.

6. The Therapeutic Stir: Consider the therapeutic nature of stirring a pot of simmering fruits or ladling hot liquid into jars. In these moments, you found solace and comfort in the rhythmic tasks of canning. Reflect on how the canning process, beyond creating culinary delights, became a therapeutic ritual fostering mental well-being and resilience.

7. Adapting to the Seasons: As you adjusted recipes based on the season's bounty, you unknowingly embraced the concept of adaptability. Reflect on how the fluidity of canning recipes mirrors life's changes. Each jar is a confirmation of your ability to adapt, a skill that extends far beyond the kitchen.

8. Jars as Milestones: Each jar can be viewed as a milestone, marking not only culinary achievements but personal growth as well. Reflect on how your canning skills have evolved over time. The novice canner who nervously sealed their first jar is now an experienced enthusiast, and each jar is a marker of that incredible journey.

9. The Joy of Sharing: Reflect on the joy derived from sharing your canned creations. The act of sharing extends beyond gifting jars; it's about fostering connection and community. Through canning, you've discovered the profound joy that comes from enriching the lives of others through your culinary creations.

10. Cultivating Gratitude: Consider the gratitude cultivated through the canning process. Each jar represents the fruits of your labor—literal and metaphorical. Reflect on the satisfaction derived from producing something valuable with your own hands, fostering a sense of gratitude for the process and the results.

11. A Jar of Endurance: Life is full of storms, and your canning journey has mirrored this truth. Reflect on the storms you weathered in the kitchen—the unexpected mishaps, the challenges of balancing ingredients, and the occasional recipe gone awry. Each jar represents your endurance, standing tall amid life's storms.

12. Seeds of Inspiration: Consider the seeds of inspiration you've sown in others. Reflect on how your canning journey has inspired friends and family to embark on their preservation

adventures. Each jar becomes a vessel of inspiration, carrying the potential to cultivate growth in those around you.

13. Future Harvests: As you reflect on the growth within each jar, let your thoughts extend to the future. Anticipate the growth yet to come—both in your canning skills and in the lessons life has in store for you. Each jar is a promise of future harvests, waiting to be savored and celebrated.

Emphasizing the ongoing nature of the canning journey, with endless possibilities for exploration

The canner's journey is not a one-time voyage but a perpetual expedition into unexplored flavors, techniques, and recipes. Each jar sets the stage for the next adventure, making your kitchen a harbor for continuous exploration. While traditional jams and pickles are the familiar shores of our canning maps, the ever-expanding ocean beckons us to venture beyond. Explore exotic spices, rare fruits, and unexpected pairings. Consider infusing your preserves with herbs or spices for a twist that takes your taste buds on a thrilling voyage.

Just as a seasoned navigator learns to read the stars, a canner masters the art of preserving through varied techniques. Try the process of fermenting, dehydrating, or even smoking your ingredients before sealing them in jars. The canning seas are teeming with techniques waiting to be discovered. Consider each jar as a point on your flavor map, creating a unique archipelago of tastes. As you experiment with ingredients and combinations, you're charting your own culinary course. Don't be afraid to let your taste buds guide the way and create your flavor paradise.

The winds of seasonal change bring with them new opportunities for exploration. From the first tender shoots of spring to the hearty produce of fall, let the changing seasons inspire your canning expeditions. Embrace the bounty of each harvest, and let your jars reflect the kaleidoscope of nature's offerings.

In the vastness of the canning sea, the lighthouse of innovation beckons. Illuminate your culinary path with creative ideas. Consider infusing your preserves with unexpected ingredients like floral notes, spirits, or even a dash of heat. Let your jars be beacons of creativity, lighting the way for other canners to follow.

Just as ships once sailed to distant lands, your jars can bridge culinary traditions. Combine ingredients from different cultures to create fusion delights. Perhaps a Moroccan-inspired chutney or a Mediterranean-infused tomato sauce. Your jars become vessels of cultural exchange, carrying the flavors of different shores. As you sail through the canning seas, amassing a bounty of flavors, don't forget to share your discoveries with your fellow mariners. Host canning gatherings where jars become tales, and recipes are shared like cherished legends. Let the canning community be a thriving port for the exchange of culinary riches.

Consider preservation as the vast ocean that encompasses canning. Explore beyond jams and pickles into the realm of canned soups, sauces, and exotic spreads. Dive into the ocean of preservation, where every jar is a treasure waiting to be discovered. Every jar has a story, much like the sunsets and sunrises at sea. Reflect on your canning horizon—the journeys taken, the lessons learned, and the flavors savored. Each jar is a snapshot of a moment in your culinary voyage.

Just as navigators of old studied the seas, a canner's education is ongoing. Immerse yourself in canning literature, attend workshops, and engage with the canning community. Let your knowledge grow like a flourishing maritime library.

The ship's galley is where culinary magic happens, but your can-do attitude extends beyond it. Approach every challenge with the spirit of a seasoned sailor. Whether it's tackling a tricky recipe or navigating a canning conundrum, let your perseverance be your compass.

Expand your canning horizons by visiting canning events and festivals. These ports of call are opportunities to exchange knowledge, taste unique creations, and connect with like-minded canners. Make these events waypoints in your canning calendar.

Celebrating Your Culinary Achievements

Sharing your creations with friends and family

Consider the joy that comes with presenting a jar of your homemade creation to a friend or family member. It's not just about the contents of the jar; it's a gesture filled with love and thoughtfulness. Explore how these simple gifts become tokens of affection and cherished moments.

Your beautifully crafted jars have the power to inspire. Sharing your creations can spark an interest in canning among your friends and family. By giving them a taste of your culinary prowess, you might just plant the seed for their own canning adventures.

Discover the art of tailoring your canned goods to suit the preferences of your recipients. Adding a personal touch, be it a special label, unique packaging, or a handwritten note, elevates the act of sharing to a personalized and memorable experience.

Reflect on the role that shared jars play in building and strengthening connections. Whether it's swapping jars with fellow canning enthusiasts or creating a tradition of gifting canned goods, explore how these jars become connectors, fostering a sense of community and shared joy.

Consider how sharing your canned goods becomes a conversation starter. Discuss about recipes, techniques, and the joy of canning. Explore how your jars initiate culinary dialogues, creating a space for shared experiences and the exchange of knowledge.

Explore the versatility of your canned creations as gifts for various occasions. Whether it's birthdays, holidays, or milestones, consider the joy that comes with presenting a jar filled with homemade goodness.

Witness how the act of sharing extends beyond your immediate circle. As your friends and family share your creations with their networks, explore the ripple effect that occurs. Your love for canning becomes a contagious enthusiasm, inspiring others to try their hand at preserving.

Reflect on the gratitude that emerges from the act of sharing. The simple act of presenting a jar can evoke heartfelt expressions of thanks. Explore the reciprocal nature of sharing, where both the giver and receiver experience a profound sense of appreciation.

Consider the joy of creating a reciprocal cycle of sharing. Encouraging your friends and family to embark on their own canning adventures completes the circle of generosity. The exchange of homemade treasures becomes a tradition that spans generations.

The journey doesn't end but continues with each jar filled

Sealing a jar is not the end of the journey—it's a prelude to more. Each lid you pop is a gateway to a world of infinite creativity, waiting for your culinary prowess to explore. Picture your pantry as a library, and each jar as a book. Closing a jar is not shutting a book; it's turning a page, revealing a new chapter in your library of flavors.

You've mastered the basics—congratulations! But in the world of home canning, mastery isn't a summit; it's a basecamp for the ascent into ever greater heights of culinary expertise. Every jar is a story, and your pantry, a library of culinary adventures. Think of each jar as a chapter in a book that's constantly evolving, each story beckoning you to explore further.

Your canning journey isn't a straight road; it's a path with forks leading to boundless exploration. Imagine flavors beyond the horizon, waiting for you to discover them. Canning is not a destination—it's an odyssey of perpetual learning. Your journey grows with each batch, each lesson becoming a stepping stone toward greater culinary heights.

Think you've covered it all? Unveil new horizons in canning—delve into recipes that go beyond the obvious, experiment, and create in ways you never thought possible. Your canning journey isn't about following a recipe; it's about embracing your can-do spirit. Transform from chef to creator, infusing each jar with your unique touch.

Passing the tongs isn't a simple handover; it's an entrustment of your culinary heritage. Share not just jars but the stories, techniques, and passion that make your canning unique. Ever thought of keeping a culinary journal? Each entry isn't just a record; it's a chronicle of flavors, a tale of your canning journey waiting to be revisited and expanded.

Canning isn't just for a season; it's a dance through time. Sync your canning rhythm with the seasons, each jar capturing a unique essence of the moment. Your canning journey isn't just for today—it's a sustainable note, a melody meant to echo through generations. Ensure your jars contribute to a culinary legacy.

Conclusion

As we reach the final pages of our "Complete Guide to Home Canning," I find myself reflecting on the aromatic odyssey we've embarked upon together. From the crisp snap of fresh produce to the gentle pop of a sealed jar, our journey has been nothing short of a flavorful masterpiece.

Think back to the beginning, where we peeled, chopped, simmered, and sealed with anticipation. Each chapter was a brushstroke, and now, we stand back to admire the beautiful fabric we've woven together—a drapery that tells the story of your growth as a home canner.

In the spirit of the harvest, we cultivated a bounty of knowledge. From understanding the nuances of preserving the perfect texture in jams to uncovering the secrets of gourmet delights, we've filled our culinary basket with insights that transcend the kitchen—lessons that enrich our lives.

Remember those unconventional spreads and unique ingredients that transformed your preserves into culinary marvels? We've shattered the boundaries of traditional canning, encouraging you to compose your flavor harmony. Your kitchen is no longer just a space for preservation; it's a stage for your creativity.

As we explored sustainability and reduced food waste, we not only lessened our environmental impact but also embraced a mindful approach to our culinary endeavors. The echo of our efforts extends beyond the jars, influencing the way we connect with the world through our kitchens.

For every challenge you faced, you emerged with newfound confidence. The troubleshooting guide became your trusted ally, transforming obstacles into stepping stones. You navigated the journey, transforming uncertainties into triumphs, instilling confidence in every aspect of your canning repertoire.

In the realm of sustainability, we delved into environmentally friendly packaging and discussed ways to reduce energy consumption—a small yet impactful contribution to our planet. Your kitchen isn't just a space for culinary artistry; it's a sanctuary for conscious, eco-friendly practices.

Our exploration into visually appealing canned goods allowed you to showcase your creations as works of art. Your kitchen transformed into a gallery, and every jar emerged as a gem ready to delight both the eyes and the palate.

As we discussed the sentimentality of gifting home-canned goods, I hope you experienced the joy of sharing pieces of your culinary heart with loved ones. Each jar became a vessel of love, a tangible expression of your passion, and a unique gift that transcends the material.

In the final chapter, we highlighted the growth and resilience gained through home canning. Your journey doesn't end; it evolves with each jar you fill. The kitchen, once a place of mere sustenance, is now a harbor of growth, resilience, and endless possibilities.

As we bid adieu to this guide, let's raise a metaphorical jar in a culinary salute. Whether you're a novice or a seasoned canner, I hope this guide has been your trusted companion, enriching your culinary repertoire and infusing your kitchen with the spirit of creativity.

This isn't a goodbye; it's a "see you later." May your jars always seal with perfection, your flavors dance harmoniously, and your kitchen remain a canvas for culinary exploration. Until our culinary paths cross again, keep savoring the journey.

www.ingramcontent.com/pod-product-compliance
Lightning Source LLC
Chambersburg PA
CBHW080929260726
48661CB00010B/3856